A PLACE IN MIND

Avi Friedman

A Place in Mind

The Search for Authenticity

Avi Friedman

Véhicule Press

Published with the generous assistance of The Canada Council for the
Arts, the Canada Book Fund of the Department of Canadian Heritage
and the Société de développement des entreprises culturelles du
Québec (SODEC).

Cover design: David Drummond
Set in Adobe Minion and Garamond by Simon Garamond
Frontispiece photo: Lucca, Italy, by Avi Friedman
Printed by Marquis Book Printing Inc.

LIBRARY AND ARCHIVES CANADA CATALOGUING IN PUBLICATION

Friedman, Avi, 1952-
A place in mind : the search for authenticity / Avi Friedman.

ISBN 978-1-55065-282-6

1. Place (Philosophy) in architecture. 2. City and town
life—Psychological aspects. 3. Architecture—Human factors.
I. Title.

NA2500.F75 2010   720.1   C2010-900768-9

Published by Véhicule Press, Montréal, Québec, Canada
www.vehiculepress.com

Distribution in Canada by LitDistCo
www.litdistco.ca

Printed in Canada on 100% post-consumer recycled paper.

In memory of my mother
Dina Piha Friedman

Contents

Departure

I WAS ACHING FROM HEAD TO TOE when I woke up, feeling feverish and drowsy. I realized that I had the flu. I returned to the comfort of my bed. Peering through the window, I saw snow drifting across the yard. On the radio, the weatherman promised a bitterly cold day. I wanted to stay home. I tried to figure out how I could avoid an afternoon meeting that I was supposed to chair at work, but I had no choice; people were coming from out of town, so I would wait a while, load myself up with tea and medicine, and venture out.

It was lunchtime when Montreal's underground Métro line brought me to my regular stop. As I made my way to the exit, I caught a glimpse of a food court in an adjacent mall and was lured by a poster featuring a steaming bowl of soup. "I should have a bowl before I head to the office," I thought, recalling the medicinal wonders attributed to chicken soup.

I approached one of the eateries, grabbed a plastic tray, and placed it on a metal counter. Oversized illuminated images showing combination dinners and their prices were featured on a back wall. I gave my order to a young man wearing a hairnet. He went to the counter, removed a lid from a large pot, and poured the contents of a ladle into a Styrofoam cup. I paid, moved to a nearby stand from which I got a plastic spoon, a packet of salt, and a few napkins, and walked to the seating area.

A row of cafeteria-like tables with seats affixed to the floor lined a wall. I noticed an empty table, removed my heavy winter gear, and squeezed myself into the gap between the table and the seat. The place started to fill up. Lunchtime patrons lined up in front of counters, got their food, and scouted for empty seats. I looked at the high ceiling. Painted black, it was daunting with exposed ducts and conduits. The sparse light fixtures cast a soft yellow shade that draped a monochrome veil over the place. It was a surreal scene— a crowd of well-dressed people, many sitting alone under dim light in the dead of winter, eating food whose culinary roots were in places half a world away.

I wondered why I disliked that place and moment. My illness was probably the root cause, I decided. My body ached, my state of mind was weak, I did not relate to the people who shared the food court, and my spirits were down. Did the *locale*, the built environment, have something to do with it? It had. It offered no comfort. It did nothing to soothe and improve my state. It failed to welcome, and lacked the touches needed to turn a passerby into a guest or resident. Designed for short-term use, it did not evoke trust and was devoid of *sense of place*. It did not offer the nurturing experience I was craving.

What do I mean by "place"? Places give the people who inhabit, visit, and use them an identity. Those with an authentic atmosphere inspire people and draw them into some kind of relationship. They are characterized by signs and symbols unique to each.

How do we assess a place? Our senses give us clues, but few places reveal their identity all at once, although we may like or dislike them in an instant. In others, we may take our time. We tend to erase the recollection of banal, unimportant spots from our thoughts and to savor the memory of others for a long time.

Places can be engaging. They can turn a passive visitor into an active participant in a life scene. A walk, or a climb, to a site with a breathtaking view can work wonders on the body. A visit to a museum can provoke ideas that inspire us. Places can evoke spiritual experiences. The red glow of a desert sunset can spark deep emotions of submission to nature's powers. Some quality in a place may put us in a mood to help foster new relationships or strengthen old ones. A chance encounter with a stranger in a small corner café may turn into a lifelong courtship.

"Good" places engage us and keep us coming back. We may stumble across them by accident or be directed there by others, but they must be experienced firsthand to be appreciated, and kept among our treasured artefacts. Special spots can be found anywhere: in a posh quarter of town or a rundown district. They can be the size of a small room or on the scale of a civic square. They can be adorned or bare, and of any shape. What makes them unique is our notice of them and their effect on us.

The search for evocative places, and wonder at the disappearance of many of them, are at the heart of this book. It is a reflection on places that touch life and affect people in positive ways. I have pondered the characteristics of such sites and have searched for the subtle and overt qualities that make us appreciate, or become disconnected from, a location.

My quest took me to spiritual places, marketplaces, walking places, very cold and warm ones, some close to home, others remote. Some made themselves known unexpectedly, and stirred questions and ideas. I went on to look into their histories. I studied their effect on civilizations and their inhabitants. I reflected on their uniqueness.

I explored the roots and the evolution of the places I discuss—stumbling onto a public market at the crack of dawn in Dalian, China triggered reflections on the value of such places in our cities. I thought about the disappearance of folk art from neighborhoods when I accidentally walked into a collection of life-sized soapstone sculptures in a Canadian Arctic town. I considered the environmental relationship between cities and their surroundings when visiting Fargo, North Dakota, on a frigid day. I reminisced about the unraveling of human relations in North America when I was taken by the warmth and camaraderie among spectators at the horse race of Casole d'Elsa in Tuscany. When I strolled through an Israeli neighborhood I was struck by the relationship between the poor state of fitness among many of the young and the disappearance of

AVI FRIEDMAN

pathways from community planning.

After sipping mint tea in an age-old teahouse in Istanbul, I thought about the evolution of building methods and reflected on the disappearance of craftsmanship. While in densely-populated Hong Kong, I wondered why we resist neighborhoods with higher densities, and I studied urban sprawl and the effect that this will have on the planet. When I dined in the kitchen of Pina and Felice in Volterra, Italy, and admired the cultivated landscape and the centuries-old buildings, I pondered the notion of, and need for, historic preservation.

What, then, is the nature of places? Why do some locations resonate more deeply within us than others? Why do we experience some places as nurturing? What is it in certain areas that fosters community—and in others that mitigates against it? What are the characteristics of a "positive" or "good" place? What lessons can they teach us that we can apply when planning future urban communities? The spots and ideas assembled here are meant to offer a looking-glass into what places are, how they came to be, and the lessons they can teach.

One

Teatime in Istanbul

I visited Istanbul, which spans two continents and touches the Sea of Marmara, on a hot summer day. I had left the Blue Mosque, still mesmerized by its stunning interiors and from time to time spotted its minarets and domes among the crowded buildings as I strolled further away. The afternoon streets were deserted and only a few shops were open, their keepers sitting in the cool indoors waiting for the odd customer. I was battling jet lag. The day had begun at Mehmet the Conqueror's Topkapi Palace and continued at the Hagia Sofia, with its thirty million gold mosaic tiles. I reflected on these treasures and pondered my next destination. The Grand Bazaar perhaps? I looked at my map: too far—I needed to pause.

In a narrow street I heard the soft chanting of eastern music. The sound came from behind an unmarked blue metal gate. I pushed it open, entered a narrow passage, took a few steps into a court between buildings, and found myself in an outdoor teahouse the size of a large North American living room.

The yard was covered by an intricate web of grapevine with plump translucent grapes dangling from gnarled branches. Sunlight flowed through the web, dappling the old cobblestone pavement. In the center was a small stone fountain; its dripping water muffled the animated conversation of the patrons. Worn plaster covered the walls, but on one side were hand-painted tiles; their intricate traditional blue and green pattern echoed the grapevine growing above.

People were sitting on sofas and stools in the shade of upper-floor balconies supported by columns. Holding glasses of tea and puffing occasionally on their *nargiles*, the traditional water pipes, they spoke to each other, punctuating their comments with hand gestures. In a corner, two men played *Shesh Besh*, backgammon, as others looking on.

A waiter, wearing a stained apron and sporting a bushy moustache, nodded to me and pointed to an empty corner sofa covered with a faded striped red rug. I sank in and stretched my legs. The man returned moments later with a low wooden stool on which he rested a steaming glass of tea with mint leaves peeking out over its edge. I sipped slowly and watched the scene. There was a sense of serenity. The colors, the grapevine, the sound of water, the murmuring of conversation and the smell all had a calming effect. Time slowed down at the Turkish teahouse.

I wondered what made the moment unique. Was it the relaxing effect of the mint tea on a tired traveler, or was it the place itself, its sounds and sights and smells? Was it perhaps something about the culture in which I was embedded? Looking at the place, I recognized how history had shaped it. It took many decades, perhaps centuries, for this small tearoom to convey the atmosphere that it did. The cobblestones had rounded edges, the grapevine adhered to the trellises, the tiles' colors were fading, the wooden stools displayed the marks of the many glasses that had rested on them, and the rug that covered the sofa on which I sat was worn and threadbare.

I found myself speculating whether the difference between Middle Eastern and Western attitudes to places has to do with our lack of patience and constant longing for instant gratification. Lifestyle trends and communication technologies have thrown us into a rush and an endless quest to keep up with things. Have those very same tendencies shortened our attention spans and affected our appreciation of places? Are we prepared to invest the time needed for a place to age and mature, a prospect that may only benefit future generations? Have we created the "architecture of the immediate", where edifices are designed and built to impress for a limited time until the next trendy style or artifact captures the limelight and casts shadows on the previous?

A scan through the history of architecture demonstrates that until the nineteenth century, styles lasted a long time, although their lifespans grew progressively shorter. There were evolutionary phases within the periods, yet the core design principles, with their identifiable elements, remained intact for centuries. Byzantine architecture, for example, began about the year 525 and lasted until 1520. Gothic architecture, and all its variations, started with the Early English Period around 1190 and ended with the Brick Gothic, *circa* 1400. Tudor style lasted about a hundred and eighteen years, and the Gothic Revival about eighty.

The duration of 20th-century styles was much shorter. The simplified design of the Bauhaus influenced architects between 1919 and the 1960s. Art Deco was in vogue in Europe and America between 1925 and 1940, Russian Constructivism from 1925 to 1932, and Postmodern architecture was a feature of the 1980s.

There are various reasons for the longevity of styles in earlier centuries. The initiators of the early large-scale edifices in Western societies were local rulers or the clergy, sometimes one and the same. Styles were first manifested in the design of religious buildings, including cathedrals and churches, or in palaces which served both as residences and as seats of government. Public buildings were constructed for prayer or governance, but also to display wealth, power, and technological superiority. Architectural advancement has often taken place with these motives.

Monarchs or religious leaders who commissioned ancient building projects probably hoped to witness their inauguration, but knew from history that, although they might never get to walk in the completed structure, their legacy would be recorded as having initiated the structures. Putting forward the funds, overseeing design, and engaging the laborers were partly egotistical acts, but they were gestures of foresight and an admirable commitment to history.

The building process was often interrupted. The patrons' deaths, dwindling funds, the rise of a new geopolitical power, and natural or man-made disasters could slow down or halt construction. Decades would pass until construction would resume, often with a new ruler at the throne and a fresh building team. A new style began when the old one ran its course with the completion of the structure.[1]

The invention of each new architectural vocabulary was founded on the footings of the old. It was a slow evolutionary process whose anchors were trial and error as well as attempts to push the envelope. Master builders learned from their predecessors' mistakes and tried to surpass their competitors' breakthroughs.

Large-scale buildings were constructed to impress; tall ceilings, grand spans and spaces, and lavish interiors were meant to draw a "wow", and leave a commoner or visiting dignitary breathless. The design challenge was often to build very tall self-supporting structures that could withstand the elements, or to create the maximum column-free space, without a roof collapse.

These were awesome undertakings, given the available scientific knowledge, construction technology, building materials, tools, and equipment. There were basically two materials. Where forests existed, or where lumber could be imported, they used wood. The other was stone or brick. Some centuries-old wood structures have lasted, but others fell victim to fire and rot. More masonry structures survived and they offer a recorded architectural history. It is impressive to note how far back stone-masonry technology, with its many variations and types, began.[2]

In the fourth millennium B.C., the Mesopotamians built palaces and places of worship of stone and sun-dried brick. In the next millennium, the Egyptians constructed stone temples and pyramids. The Greeks mastered limestone and marble carving technique in the first century B.C. The Greek skill was inherited by the Romans, who went on to develop arches and roof vaults that were included in their own impressive structures. Knowledge accumulated by the Romans was perfected by medieval civilizations in the Occident and in the Islamic world, where beautiful buildings faced with glazed tiles, much like the ones that I saw in Istanbul, were constructed. Later centuries in Europe saw the construction of fortresses and cathedrals of stone. Buttresses were invented during the Gothic era. Masonry was also masterfully used by other civilizations in Central and South America and Asia.[3]

Employing masonry in building demanded advanced skills. Rudimentary design and drafting practices required enormous accuracy, as pieces were prefabricated on the ground and hoisted into place. Arches and vaults were made of many different-sized components, each with its own angles, that when lifted and put together had to fit perfectly. Stone pieces will not meet each other unless they have been pre-constructed with utmost accuracy.

The building process began when a designer/master-builder, the forefather of today's architect, was invited to conceive and supervise construction of an edifice. It has often been stated that bishops and monks were the architects. The master-builder hired a team of master craftsmen who worked under him. There were quarry-men, stonecutters, sculptors, mortar-makers, masons, carpenters, blacksmiths, roofers, and glassmakers, each of whom ran his own trade. They were assisted by apprentices who, in turn, supervised unskilled laborers.

Work proceeded with manual labor and basic tools. Animals transported large slabs of stone from quarries to a mason's shop. There they would be reduced to size and hand-carved to fit a dimension indicated on the master-builder's drawing. The finished piece would be transported to the building site where it would be hoisted in place by hand-operated cranes and scaffolding, to become part of a wall, a column, or an arch. The notion "built to last" was evident in all stages of work. Craftsmen knew that their creation would endure. Their legacies were these edifices, into which they sometimes carved their own likenesses for all to see.

The construction of a single edifice took many years, and involved hundreds or even thousands of craftsmen and laborers. Construction of Westminster Abbey, for example, started in 1045 and ended around 1400. The building of Florence's cathedral, which was designed by Arnofo di Cambio, began in 1296 and ended in 1462. San Giorgio Maggiore, one of Andrea Palladio's masterpieces in Venice, was built between 1560 and 1580, a relatively short time.

The Industrial Revolution altered architecture. New materials as well as advanced structural calculations and mechanized modes were developed; they sped up production and shortened construction time. Labor-intensive cut stone, for example, lost its place as a prime structural material with the invention of Portland cement by Joseph Aspdin in England in 1824.[3] Cement permitted the creation of "artificial stone" that, when poured into molds, hardened in a few days to form a lasting structural component. A patent was obtained in 1867 by French gardener Joseph Mounier for a combination of steel and cement; reinforced concrete changed construction methods and the history of architecture.

Wide-span beams, large-expanse floor slabs, and earthquake-resistant tall buildings could now be constructed rapidly. Cement mixers, cranes, and power tools became widespread. Advancements in the production of other materials like glass and steel and their proliferation and ease of use helped to push cut stone aside as a prime structural and cladding product. Although construction technology improved remarkably, the new materials lacked the longevity of the old. Glass curtain walls, with their intricate details, were not meant to last centuries. There was a time limit on how long the new materials could last. The initiators of these buildings assumed that a few decades following the end of construction, the building's outer skin would have to undergo extensive maintenance or be replaced.

Successive technological advancements have introduced new building systems. Heating, ventilation, air conditioning, humidity control, security, and sprinklers have become permanent features of large-scale buildings. They run their course and need to be replaced when they reach the end of their useful life expectancy or when a more advanced system is invented. Buildings and their components are designed to be modified and changed. The notion of a building lasting several centuries does not hold in this era of constant advancements. Limited use, common in consumption of personal goods, has to a certain degree found its way into architecture.

Architecture as we know it was a fledgling profession at the turn of the nineteenth century. Architects included in their designs details drawn from pattern books and catalogues of machine-made products. Some craftsmen went to work in factories while the skills of others were rendered obsolete. Centuries-old traditions that had been passed on from one generation to the next were lost. There was less need for master glassmakers, blacksmiths, or stonecutters.

The diminished need for craftsmanship paralleled another milestone in architectural history: the dawn of the Modern Movement at the turn of the 20th century. Historians trace the movement's beginning to the Bauhaus, a German school of design and architecture founded in 1919 and headed by Walter Gropius. Bauhaus architects favored functional design choices that kept costs down. Rejecting articulated stone facades, elaborate wood detailing, ornate metal cornices, eaves, and other decorative details, they employed principles of classical architecture in its simplest and purest form. Flat roofs, square building shapes, and plain furniture were some of the Bauhaus trademarks. There were fewer features on the building facade and interior to age gracefully.

With the rise of Nazism in the 1930s, the school shut down and its founders moved to America. The movement transformed and was renamed the International Style after the 1932 book, *The International Style*, written by historian Henry-Russell Hitchcock and architect Philip Johnson, which was published to accompany a Museum of Modern Art exhibition.[4]

International Style buildings were meant to be simple and, in the case of residences, affordable to the masses.

Through time, the context of building has altered. Most notable was the rise of the speculator in construction.[5] Speculation has been present throughout urban history, but whereas religious, government, and upscale residential buildings were initiated and funded by rulers and the clergy, homes not built by their occupants were the products of speculation. In cities, master-builders would purchase a lot on which they would construct a single or multifamily dwelling structure for sale or rent. A walk through cities like Paris or Amsterdam draws admiration for the attention that was paid by speculators to their buildings, with intricate brickwork, decorated rooftops, and stained-glass windows as part of the vocabulary.

The Industrial Revolution gave rise to a new type of speculative building. Corporations that produced and sold goods offered services and managed assets needed office space in bustling cities. The modern office building, where spaces were rented to companies, became the norm.

The Modern Movement offered an advantage to speculators. Whereas a great deal of craftsmanship at large expense was an innate aspect of old structures, there was no need for it in the speculative building of the twentieth century. The stripped-down facades and boxy edifices sprang up in cities and suburbs. Their main purpose was to turn a profit on investment in a short time, while satisfying their tenants' basic needs. Suitable urban design, good architecture, and fine craftsmanship were replaced by plain buildings that had no relation to their location.

Loss of context was a contributor to the diminishment of sense of place. In the Istanbul teahouse, I was surrounded by the markings of a place. The tiles affixed to the wall were made by local artisans and were based on traditional motifs which were also present in the rug that upholstered the couch on which I was seated and the stool where my glass of tea rested. They were all crafted locally and formed part of the place, along with other cultural insignia. The backgammon boards, the hookahs, and the animated conversations created an expression unique to the culture of an Istanbul neighborhood.

Modern communication and the rise of the digital age have served to erode the contextual dimension. Buildings of any style can now be constructed anywhere. It is still preferable that they fit in with their specific urban contexts, but it is no longer a mandatory requirement handed to their architects. There is no longer a perceived need to integrate markings of local cultures through use of materials, the work of artisans, and the inclusion of local living norms. Same-style buildings can now be constructed in countries continents apart. Celebrated architects are being invited to design buildings, in their trademark style, everywhere. The Los Angeles-based Frank O. Gehry, known for his zinc-clad curvy exteriors, has designed similar-looking buildings in Los Angeles, Frankfurt, Paris, Bilbao, Kobe, and Prague.

Whereas in the past, knowledge of a new building and familiarity with the intricacies of its details took years to cross territorial boundaries and continents, they now do so quickly. Images of structures under construction or just completed can now be easily published in a newspaper or magazine, shown on television, and posted on websites for all to see and emulate. The pace of cross-border architecture and of change in styles has accelerated.

Western society's norms are changing as well. The end of the twentieth century and the dawn of the twenty-first moved us into a faster mode. We are constantly catching up with the endless outpouring of new information and gaining familiarity with the next technology. The rushed pace has shortened our attention span and taken away the patience needed to appreciate things, let them age properly, and mentally digest them. Many are not willing to invest the necessary time to know things, buildings among them, intimately. We are in a constant search for new personal and artistic gratification. But by contrast, strangely enough, we have developed uncommon relationships with the old. We travel to faraway destinations in our own country or abroad, to appreciate and soak in the aroma of centuries past. We visit antique markets in search of a perfect old chest of drawers, yet we are often not willing to take part in preserving the old in our own backyard or to give a place the time needed to grow and age.

Sitting on the couch and sipping tea at the Istanbul teahouse helped me recognize that for a place to offer a unique sense of itself requires time. It is not only a matter of years, but also of a holistic approach that begins by choosing a proper design and materials that will age gracefully. Today, unfortunately, we build places which will never age; they will simply be rendered obsolete, ready for demolition.

My experience in the teahouse reminded me, too, that to appreciate a place, I need to slow down and take time to read its revealing marks and to allow its hidden language to speak.

Two

Fiore di Zucchini in Montepulciano

THE SETTING SUN CAST AN ORANGE LIGHT on the medieval buildings that framed Piazza Grande in the Tuscan town of Montepulciano as my wife and I walked across the square in front of the Palazzo Comunale. There was no activity, except for a flock of doves that struggled to grab bread crumbs from an old man's palm. The town hall had an imposing tower. Beside it was the cathedral, with its plain facade. Montepulciano was built around 1511 for Cosimo I, along a narrow limestone ridge. Renaissance-style *palazzi* and store-fronts with apartments above lined the narrow curved streets leading to the hilltop. Signs directed visitors to the many wine stores where Montepulciano's famous *vino nobile* was sold.

It was getting dark when we checked into Il Riccio, a *palazzo* turned hotel, built on the edge of the cliff. From our room we watched the sun set over a magnificent tapestry of cultivated land.

We were tired and hungry after driving all day along snaky roads, and began to look for a place to dine. Sounds and aromas from open upper-floor windows signaled that the locals were getting ready to have supper. I asked a young woman if she could direct us to a fine restaurant. She said that the choice was limited in this small town, then pointed to the Osteria Acquacheta on Via del Teatro, a place that she frequented. *Mangia bene, paga giusto* ("reasonably priced good food"), she added in Italian.

The Osteria was crowded. The air was perfumed with a blend of grilled meat, balsamic vinegar, oregano, and red wine. The patrons seemed to be mostly locals. After a short wait, a lanky, ponytailed man wearing blue jeans and sandals greeted us. He explained that in this small establishment, there were only tables for four and that we would be seated with another couple.

I was tired, hungry, and in no mood to rub elbows with strangers. We whispered to each other, considered our options, and realized that they were few. I nodded to the man, who directed us to a table, half of which was occupied by a young couple who were chatting quietly in Italian.

Bread and an uncorked bottle of house wine were brought to the table, along with a hand-written menu. Minutes later, the man returned, described some of the menu items, and took our orders. The long and narrow space had vaulted ceilings and was tucked under an old four-story stone building. Approximately twelve tables of four were lined up next to the walls, leaving a narrow passage in between. It felt as if we had walked into an Italian version of a Brueghel painting because the patrons' gestures and expressions were animated and the mood joyous. In the rear, the kitchen was raised somewhat above the main level with no separation from the dining area. A woman of a certain age was busy cooking, helped by a boy. Using wooden pallets, he slid metal plates in and out of a wood-burning oven.

We waited quietly, peering at the dishes served to adjacent tables. After a few exchanges of smiles, the couple with whom we shared a table introduced themselves. We told them where we were from, and they replied that they lived in Ravenna in northern Italy and that they were on vacation. The woman was an art restorer of Czech heritage, and her husband an engineer. They had met by chance on his visit to Prague, she explained.

Fiore di zucchini (stuffed zucchini flowers) was the appetizer, followed by *zuppa di fagioli*, a white bean soup, then *stufato alla fiorentina* (beef in red wine).

The place was working its magic. I felt relaxed, and wondered what made the moment special. Was it the soothing effect of exquisite food and wine on a hungry traveler, or the unexpected pleasure of meeting, sharing experiences, and dining with strangers? The place, I felt, with all its attributes, had a lot to do with it. The seating arrangement, the absence of tablecloths on the scratched wooden tabletops, the centuries-old exposed brick and stone walls, the arched ceiling, the rustic tiled floor, and the open kitchen all seemed authentic, along with the moment itself. Nothing in what we were experiencing seemed to have been choreographed or planned. The simplicity of the venue, the welcoming manners, and the gestures of kindness of the people who cooked and served were naturally woven into the scene.

Restaurants like the one we enjoyed in Montepulciano are harder to find nowadays. In large cities, many have fallen victim to savvy, well-advertised establishments part of multi-outlet chains. Why and how did it happen? Will the evolution of public dining and changes in our own habits and attitudes likely contribute to the disap-pearance of these unique places?

Inns, taverns, and *traiteurs* (cookshops) were the forerunners of restaurants. They emerged as people traveled more. The need for places to feed and water passengers and horses on long voyages brought them about. In the eleventh century country inns were established by monks to shelter pilgrims. Monastic hospices that offered food, drink, and stables were fixtures of several continents.[1]

Known as *Kahn* throughout the Middle East, early inns had an interior court surrounded by a stone building, often with a colonnade. The lower level housed public functions, and accommodations were available on the floor above. A splendid example is the *Kahn* in Acre, Israel, which has lasted to this day. It was built to welcome caravans that stopped en route between Europe and Africa.

Because they were located at junctions where people with news from afar intersected, inns attracted locals as well. They came to spend time, eat, and be informed and entertained. Dining was simple, resembling today's *table d'hôte*; patrons paid for a seat at a table which included a meal. Much like Osteria Acquacheta, inns had simple interiors and offered rudimentary comfort in a large space that accommodated both dining and cooking areas.[1]

For centuries, pubs and taverns offered drinks, but also basic food. A factor that attracted patrons was the fear of drinking polluted, disease-spreading water. Known also as "alehouses", they spread quickly throughout Europe to become a permanent feature of towns and villages. They were common in England; patrons could be served a variety of spirits. Pubs and taverns saw a decline towards the end of the eighteenth century, when their monopoly to sell wine was revoked.

Established in Europe along with the arrival of coffee from the Middle East and Ottoman Turkey, the first public coffeehouses were opened in Marseilles and Paris around 1670. They served primarily hot beverages and pastries. According to Bethan Ryder's *Restaurant Design*, in England coffeehouses started up around the same time. They were "domains where political, economic and literary issues of the day would be discussed and debated by gentlemen from all walks of life."[2] A typical coffeehouse had large windows, walls covered with wood paneling, and tables, stools, and benches. Upscale establishments had chairs upholstered in leather. They opened in other cities, including Hamburg and Amsterdam, and crossed the Atlantic. The first one in North America opened in Boston.

Coffeehouses introduced an air of civility and segregated people by social and economic class. Wealthy, educated patrons could gather to discuss cultural and business matters.

Coffeehouses were a preliminary to the introduction of restaurants, which made their first appearance in Paris in 1760. The elimination of rules set by guilds that restricted tradespeople to a single activity—bakers could not sell sandwiches, for example—paved the way for the introduction of restaurants. The first establishments served *bouillon*, a dish which was offered to restore people's health. They offered other restorative items, such as fruit, dairy products, and sweets. When a shop owner named Boulanger began, in 1765, to offer other dishes, he was sued by the *traiteurs* for breaking local commerce laws. Boulanger won. His new dishes earned him fame as well as many patrons. Other establishments followed in his footsteps by expanding their menus.[2] Restaurants began to distinguish themselves from other eating and drinking establishments by displaying menus with prices. They had flexible operating hours. The interior décor of restaurants was different, with mirrors and landscape paintings. Candles were placed on tables, private sitting rooms made available for special guests, and food served on china.[3]

In the late eighteenth century, restaurants became the bourgeois public sphere. They played a role in the development of modern structures of government, as the venue in which new political ideas, philosophies, and artistic endeavors originated. Unlike cafés, restaurants were places to which women were not only welcome, but also explicitly invited, and therefore places that better mirrored society at large. They introduced semi-public spaces, as patrons could sit at separate tables and carry on private conversations. China had restaurants before Europe did. It has been established that in the thirteenth century, restaurants in Hangzhou, then the country's capital, provided individual service and pricing to patrons. Whereas taverns sold a limited selection of food, restaurants offered a great variety, including cooking in the styles and tastes of their own and other regions.[4]

Technological developments, particularly those that were introduced from about 1800 in Europe, contributed to the expansion of restaurants. Modern lighting was one such invention. Few activities took place outside the home after dark in pre-industrial Europe. Walking in the evening, primarily in rural areas where dark was nearly absolute, was dangerous. The invention of the oil lamp in 1783 by the Swiss Ami Argand enabled cities to light streets and other public places. Argand's invention was cumbersome at first, due to the high cost of vegetable oil, but it improved when paraffin was introduced. In 1847 natural gas was introduced on a large scale. Gaslight became a fixture of many streets and public places in large cities like Paris. Going out after dark became less risky for individuals and families, and allowed the extension of restaurants' operating hours. Thomas Alva Edison's invention of the light bulb in 1879 brought further improvement and accessibility. It was coupled with a technological leap forward that occurred in 1900 when electricity was introduced as the centerpiece of the Parisian

World Exhibition. Expensive at first, electricity powered a few establishments like the modern café-restaurant Die Port van Cleve in Amsterdam.[5] Unlike gas, which elevated the temperature of a locale, electrical illumination provided light alone. Eating out grew in popularity along with the safety and comfort of diners indoors and out.

Development of food technology altered the course of restaurants' offerings. The 1810 invention of food preservation in glass jars by Nicolas Appert, a Frenchman, meant that chefs no longer had to rely entirely on seasonal products in crafting their menus. Commonly preserved items were spinach, green peas, and green beans. Preserving meant some loss of freshness. In the 1880s artificial refrigeration and freezing techniques became technically and economically possible through methods based on evaporation using compressed ammonia. Food products had a longer storage life, avoiding the threat of financial loss from unconsumed food that had to be discarded.

Along with technological innovations, new organizational ideas changed the nature of public dining. The cafeteria was introduced after World War I because of the need to serve large numbers of meals and snacks to office or factory employees over a short break. It was a new type of dining style. Having people walk along food counters and select pre-made items, or be served directly, helped to lower costs by allowing the use of unskilled staff, avoiding service to tables, and offering a relatively small selection of items. Cafeterias benefited from earlier inventions like canned food and refrigeration. They spread to many North American workplaces with large numbers of employees. Their downside was the reduction in human contact between servers and patrons that people had enjoyed in coffeehouses and restaurants. Efficiency, timesaving, and the financial bottom line were beginning to take center stage as factors in public dining.

Cafeterias ushered in another trend that would change the nature of public dining once more. Fast food was the outcome of social trends, technological innovation, and organizational methods.

The concept, introduced in the mid-1950s, was based on a highly rationalized system of factory-produced food where identical portions could be made, frozen, and shipped to outlets where they would be heated and served.

Percy Spencer's invention of the microwave oven, an outcome of experiments with magnetrons for military applications, was instrumental in food processing as it helped thaw frozen products or heat cold items rapidly. The first microwave ovens were cumbersome and expensive, but they became common features in most dining establishments and made their way into domestic kitchens.[5]

Fast food outlets prospered due to shifts in the way North Americans, and to a lesser degree, Europeans, lived their lives and housed themselves. In the 1950s, fast food outlets became fairly common in urban areas, but the majority were freestanding structures near or on arterial roads or highways. The introduction of mass production is attributed to Ray Kroc, who in the mid-1950s sold milkshake makers. Impressed by one of his clients, who ordered six machines to serve many people at once, he drove to California where he watched with amazement how the owners of a small fast-food outlet named McDonald's served large crowds. He decided to take over the franchise. Kroc's success bred imitations, and other chains soon followed.[6]

Patrons drove to fast food outlets. They either parked and ate indoors, or lined up to be served in their cars. In both cases, service was highly efficient, with chains priding themselves on being able to reduce wait-times significantly.

North Americans began to eat more and more meals away from home. Between 1977 and 1995, for example, the share of total calories consumed in restaurants in the U.S. rose from 18 to 34 per cent, the share of meals consumed in restaurants rose from 16 to 29 per cent, and the total restaurant share of food dollars rose from 26 to 39 percent.[7]

Eating establishments began to lose the vital ingredient of being a local social hub where neighbors could meet each other informally. Fast food outlets attempted to regain this, and to increase profit, by introducing play structures for toddlers within the outlet. They began to host children's birthday parties.

Another development that helped popularize fast food consumption was the evolution in shopping patterns, particularly the proliferation of the mall. As commerce was no longer economically viable directly within low-density suburban communities, residents had to drive to a place which could accommodate many shoppers. Food courts, which combine cafeteria-style service, fast food, and a shared dining area, became the hallmark of North American malls. They attempted, with little success, to offer diners cheerful environments in a noisy ambiance, epitomizing the age of speed and convenience. They expanded their reach into urban malls, where office employees had their lunch, and into airports, where travelers could eat prior to takeoff.

In 2000, U.S. customers dined out in record numbers, spending $1 billion dollars a day, according to the National Restaurant Association, up 5 percent from 1999.[8]

As dining out became routine, restaurants were transformed by catering to narrower niche markets, including families, sports fans, business people, or young crowds. International chains employed global chefs. Establishments like the Hard Rock Café or Planet Hollywood engaged celebrity designers to create a theme look.

When asked by Michael Kaplan, author of *Theme Restaurants*, what elements he had incorporated in the design of an international chain, architect David Rockwell answered, "You want them to have similar elements, so they're a part of a family. They need to have certain features that people might expect and look forward to. With Planet Hollywood, it's the memorabilia, it's the diorama, the lighting concept, the deep-blue sky effect on the ceiling. Within, you have special features that are a little less expected. In Washington, D.C., we have a war room. In London, we have a James Bond room. In Paris, there is a film noir room."[9]

In an effort to encourage repeat visits and increase market share and profits, some restaurants employed a variety of design tactics that appealed to their core customers' tastes and psychological needs, such as the desire for personal space or stimulation.[10] Designs began to employ halogen lights in trendy fixtures or to hang television screens on the walls to create unique experiences. Bright color schemes were toned down and replaced by textures.

Blue Velvet is a Los Angeles restaurant-lounge designed by brothers Mandi and Mehdi Rafaty, principles of Tag Front. The space is divided into a series of distinct areas with sliding panels and doors. According to *Interior Design* magazine, the architects gave Blue Velvet a unique look, with blue and gray wool-covered walls, anodized aluminum panels, and rectangular blocks glowing with fluorescent lights. "When light from outside shines through it, it dapples a grey wrap-around banquette and blued steel tables."[11] In their drive to distinguish one spot from another, interior designers turned things grotesque with look-alike places where lights made it hard to see one's companion, blasting music made it difficult to carry on a conversation, and oversized plates crowded the table.

What makes for a good gathering and dining place? Why did Osteria Aquacheta strike a chord? In *The Great Good Place*, Ray Oldenburg refers to sites that are not associated with dwelling or work as *third places*.[12] These are locations where we can walk away from daily habits, regimented routines, and even our own usual self. They are not part of an international chain, nor are they the sites of exquisite gourmet dining. Oldenburg suggests that one can distinguish them from other dining or gathering establishments. He offers some characteristics.

People who patronize a third place are not tied to a particular schedule and they are welcome to come and leave as they please. Third places are levelers. Patrons' wealth, social status, or even educational background are of secondary importance. "(T)he charm and flavor of one's personality, irrespective of his or her station in life, is what counts."[11]

Conversations in third places are lively, colorful, and engaging. Being attentive to others, consideration of each other's feelings, talking about topics of interest to all make for a lively exchange. The noise level and the choice of background music must allow everyone to listen and talk in a normal tone of voice. They are places to which one can go alone at any time of the day or evening and be pretty sure that an acquaintance will be present. The regulars set a tone of conviviality that makes a stranger feel welcome.

Much like my Montepulciano spot, a typical third place may be plain and unimpressive looking. You will rarely find them advertised or posting a flashy sign, because the locals know where they are. They are often independently operated, mom-and-pop businesses. Their interiors may be worn and even shabby, yet they are kept clean by owners who are devoted to the comfort of their patrons. The mood tends to be playful. Walk in and you will feel at home.

Osteria Acquacheta was a third place. Much like the simple ingredients that made our meal great, memorable third places feed their patrons a plate full of simplicity with an open heart and good will.

Three

Crowding in Hong Kong

~

THE RIDE FROM THE INTERNATIONAL AIRPORT to downtown Hong Kong was quite deceiving. The bus rolled along a serene, sparsely-populated coastal highway carved into hillsides. A while later, in a sharp transition, the blue and green turned into a gray built-up urban landscape and the sea breeze changed to stale, hot, humid air.

It grew dark as the bus edged slowly forward along clogged traffic arteries. The night offered a backdrop to the endless array of neon signs of all sizes and shades. The signs overwhelmed Nathan Lane Road, Kowloon Peninsula's main thoroughfare, where tall buildings seemed to lean on each other's shoulders and people jammed sidewalks. Looking at the crowded streets, I wondered if I had arrived on a festive night, but I quickly learned that I had not. Hong Kong is a small island with many people. You realize how precious the space is when you check into your hotel room, where every square inch is carefully planned and meticulously used.

In the morning, I made my way to the port and boarded the ferry to Hong Kong Island. As the coast approached, I recognized architect Sir Norman Foster's Bank of Hong Kong building and I. M. Pei's tall, sleek Bank of China tower. Elbowing my way in a thick crowd, I strolled through a web of narrow streets and lanes lined with shops. It was already hot. Merchants opened shutters and unlocked front doors, patrons came to shop, and tourists hunted for the perfect pearl necklace. I climbed a set of stairs with stalls piled high with watches, sunglasses, exotic fruits, and clothing on either side. I continued my walk uphill until I reached a

36

lookout of sorts and it was there that I first saw them.

A row of massive residential building blocks lay below. They were huge, a city block long, sixteen stories tall, bunched together in close formation. I could spot balconies with laundry hung to dry in some and greenery in pots in others, while many were sealed with glazing or shutters.

These were examples of Hong Kong's public rental housing, built for families who could not afford adequate, very expensive, private accommodation. There are 650,000 rental flats in the authority's portfolio, lodging approximately two million people— about a third of the territory's population of 6,864,000. The island is one of the most crowded places on earth, with some 16,300 people per square mile (6,294 people per square kilometer), compared to the United States, which has 76.25 people per square mile (29.44 people per square kilometer), and Canada, with 8.70 people per square mile (3.36 people per square kilometer).[1]

Looking at the huge buildings in the distance, I wondered what it was like to reside in them. How did their occupants cope with noise, ventilation, garbage collection, and parking, for example? Hong Kong, I realized, had no choice in sheltering its people. The sea and the mountains imposed geographic limits on its ability to spread out, creating a natural barrier which prohibited urban sprawl. I began to think about reasons why we Westerners resist higher densities and are willing to bear the consequences of urban sprawl, including longer drive times, more pollution, and social isolation. Does ease with living in close quarters have to do with a particular culture or era in history? Can it be learned? I wondered if we would ever come to our senses and accept a level of density suitable to the challenges that we are faced with.

Density, a numerical indicator of how crowded a place is, made its formal appearance along with the introduction of planning control mechanisms. Cities wanted to regulate the number of built structures and, as a consequence, the number of people who would reside or work in a given place. One of the measures, gross density, divides the number of dwellings by the development's land, which includes streets and parks. Floor-area ratio, another index, looks at how well the lot is used by counting the habitable enclosed space on all floors of a given structure and dividing it by the lot area. A downtown skyscraper will have, for example, a much higher floor-area ratio than a single-story small suburban shopping strip, despite the fact that both have a similar footprint. Densities can be measured according to the number of people who congregate in a particular place, an outcome of the number of dwelling units or work spaces.

Currently, 60 percent of North Americans reside in typical suburbs, with wide roads and single-family homes on large lots. The average density is 3,500 people per square mile (1,350 people per square kilometer). A city whose streets are lined with row houses and two-family homes, like Baltimore or Washington, D.C., will have about 10,000 people per square mile (3,900 people per square kilometer). Large metropolises like Tokyo, São Paulo, or New York's Manhattan Island have at least 100,000 people per square mile (39,000 people per square kilometer); they have tall buildings, bustling streets, congested roads, and fewer green areas.[2] Each of these locations offers a unique sense of place and engages its residents and visitors differently.

Senses of place were altered significantly in the past century. In 1820 only 7 percent of Americans lived in cities, with the majority residing in either New York or Philadelphia. Only ten cities in the U.S. could boast populations greater than ten thousand. North America at this time was not an urban continent. As the Industrial Revolution spread from England throughout the world, urban populations skyrocketed. By 1860 New York City had over one million residents, and seven other cities had populations that exceeded 100,000. By 1890 New York was approaching the size of London, while Philadelphia and Chicago were each home to a million residents. Half of all the people in the northeastern United States had become urban, as had a third of America's entire population.[3]

How did North American suburbs, with their low density and unique street patterns, come to be? Pre-Industrial Revolution cities had easily definable spatial characteristics. These included very high densities and clearly drawn limits. Mixed land uses provided people with the luxury of living close to their workplaces; often, the most respectable addresses were at the city's core. With industrialization came a change in the prioritization of urban spaces. When industries moved into the downtown areas to access cheap immigrant labor and transportation hubs, the resulting noise, dirt, and density greatly damaged the livability of many cities. It is no surprise that before urban reformers began working to extricate the working masses from crowded living conditions, exodus from the city was an option only for the rich.

Expensive and limited steam railroad lines provided a means of travel between the city and wealthy enclaves which were developed at the periphery of towns. The earliest of these enclaves, such as Llewellyn Park, New Jersey, planned in 1853, and Riverside, Illinois (1869), were novel residential experiences. Often designed by landscape architects, the neighborhoods had gently curving streets that conformed to natural topography and created idyllic settings. Picturesque homes, on lots much larger than average twentieth-century suburban lots were designed to emphasize the communities' decidedly non-urban image.[4] The early suburban homes strove to represent a new domestic ideal. They combined a careful treatment of outdoor spaces with images of European cottages.

In public opinion, the suburb gradually replaced the city as the desired place to raise a family. It took, however, a series of transportation innovations to provide accessibility for the middle class. The horse-drawn omnibus was introduced to New York City in 1829 and the horse-car in 1852. Both of these means of transport accelerated cross-town travel and made commuting socially acceptable to the general population. For the vast majority, however, the electric streetcar was the key to the suburbs. First successfully introduced in the United States in 1887, this rapid, inexpensive, and manure-free mode of transportation finally enabled the middle class to move beyond the confines of the city on a daily basis.[3]

Land speculators, many of whom also owned streetcar companies, dictated the course of early suburban development. Transit tycoons made fortunes by buying land outside the city limits and bringing the streets to it. Convenient access to downtown became a major selling point and assured future development of the site. The foreseeable result of this private speculative development was sprawl. To ensure a profitable volume of commuters, streetcar suburbs required a fairly high density. In fact, they initially resembled housing of a more urban type, simply removed from the urban setting. A typical American home along an established transportation corridor sat on a 1/10-acre (0.04-hectare) lot. Often these early suburbs were designed as an extension of the grid pattern of an existing inner city, and though the houses were detached, they were identical with those in the city core.[5] Although these developments differed substantially from the more affluent suburbs, they provided an attainable form of the domesticity and household privacy that the middle class sought.

The First World War drew a great number of farm workers to urban areas across North America. Following the war there was a suburban construction boom. In the United States, housing starts increased by nearly 10 percent annually in the 1920s, and by 1930, 48 percent of American households owned their own homes.[6]

The car gradually became a permanent fixture of the middle-class lifestyle. Initially, acceptance of the automobile had been somewhat reserved. It was viewed as a glamorous toy for the well-to-do. In 1898, for example, there was only one car per eighteen thousand people in the United States. Lack of infrastructure and service facilities, as well as the fact that cars frequently scared the horses which then dominated city streets, inhibited their popularity. As the automobile became increasingly convenient, however, the pace of acceptance naturally accelerated. Primarily because of the affordability and tremendous popularity of Henry Ford's Model T, by 1913 the ratio of cars to people in the United States had increased to one in eight. In 1925, Ford's factories produced nine thousand cars per day, and by 1927 the United States was home to twenty-six million cars. The American government responded with new policies, technology, and taxes to implement a highway system which grew into the transit arteries of American daily life.[3] The situation improved significantly and became formalized in an effort to house the population as well.

Prior to the devastation of the Great Depression, American and Canadian governments believed that housing was essentially the responsibility of the free market. Pressure for housing assistance and economic recovery during the 1930s compelled politicians to reconsider this position. In the U.S., the National Housing Act, which created the Federal Housing Administration in 1934, guaranteed mortgages, and eased the pressure of the demand for housing. The FHA agreed to insure long-term fully amortized mortgages provided by private lenders. This expanded accessibility to housing by reducing the lenders' risks, increasing their willingness to lend while limiting their down payment requirements and interest rates.[6] These terms opened home ownership to the working class. The suburban family with a new house and a long-term mortgage became the symbol of the North American way for all classes. The flip side of institutionalized suburbanization was the loss of middle-class citizens and middle-class stability in the city center.

During World War II resources and labor were diverted from housing production. Would-be home buyers had to put their aspirations on hold. Rampant post-war consumerism coupled with the great number of returning military personnel and the baby boom that followed created a terrific housing demand. In the U.S.A. and Canada, demand for housing was reinforced by the government's decision that military personnel should return to civilian life with homes of their own.[3] The most conservative estimates indicated that responding to the need would immediately require the construction of five million new units, and a total of twelve and a half million over the following decade.[7]

The American Veterans Administration in 1944 created a mortgage guarantee program as part of the GI Bill of Rights. It bolstered demand for owner-occupied units by enabling veterans to borrow the entire appraised value of a house.[7]

Estimates of the number of houses that were likely to be built made it clear that the traditional practice of housing construction by numerous small-scale builders would be insufficient for the task. The government responded with programs that made it profitable for developers to build by mass-production methods, on vast tracts of land. For the first time in history, large-scale construction companies did the majority of construction. By 1949, for example, 70 percent of new homes were built by only 10 percent of the firms.[3]

The widespread popularity of the car enabled large-scale sprawling developments. The U.S. government facilitated dependency on the car with the Interstate Highway Act of 1956, which established a trust fund through which federal authorities paid 90 percent of state and local expressway construction costs. This came as a terrible blow to the public transit system, and its use has declined steadily since that time.[8] The presence of the automobile has not been quite so overpowering in Canada. The U.S. has four times as many lane miles of urban expressway per capita, and the number of cars per capita has consistently been about 50 per cent higher.[9] Overall, Canadian cities have more viable public transportation systems and there is less deterioration in the downtown cores, yet Canadian suburban sprawl has been extensive.

The direct effect of the automobile on the planning of suburban subdivisions is evident in the switch from grid to hierarchical road networks for reasons of safety. In the mid-1950s, traffic engineering studies demonstrated that the accident rate was substantially higher for grid-pattern subdivisions than for cul-de-sac subdivisions by a ratio of almost eight to one. T-intersections were found to be fourteen times safer than four-leg intersections. The American Institute of Traffic Engineers promoted revised standards including limited access to the perimeter highway, avoidance of long local streets to discourage through traffic, and numerous three-leg T-intersections.[10,11] These standards were widely adopted and their imposition by municipal governments has made it difficult to implement new design approaches to suburban developments.

With low-density planning practices and ample roads, North

American homes have become dependent on private motor vehicles. According to Schwela and Zali, the number of vehicles on the continent increased from 52 million in 1950 to 450 million 1994.[1] This has contributed to decreased use of public transit and cutbacks in services.[13] The growing number of vehicles entails health risks. Although the composition of motor vehicle exhaust varies according to the type of fuel, the primary constituents that pose health risks are present throughout the world. Carbon monoxide, nitrogen dioxide, ozone, photochemical oxidants, and suspended particulate matter all contribute to the deterioration of air quality. Nitrogen dioxide can lead to respiratory complications such as reduced efficacy of lung defences. Carbon monoxide hinders the transportation of oxygen from the blood into the body's tissues, requiring more blood to circulate to deliver the equivalent amount of oxygen.[12]

Emissions from motor vehicles pose an imminent threat to the general environment. Between 70 and 90 percent of carbon monoxide emissions in most cities comes from motor vehicles. Cars contribute to the greenhouse effect, and in turn to climate change, through the release of carbon dioxide, methane, and nitrous oxide. Road transport accounts for 15 to 20 percent of carbon dioxide emissions worldwide.[14]

Despite the health and environmental risks, many North Americans still purchase large cars, such as minivans and sport utility vehicles. During the oil crisis of the 1970s, many consumers opted for higher efficiency vehicles with smaller engines, but as fuel prices stabilized in the 1990s, the popularity of larger cars increased. According to a Natural Resources Canada 2005 report on energy efficiency trends in Canada, performance levels, or horsepower, of the average car owned by Canadians increased by 32 percent, from 118 horsepower in 1990 to 156 horsepower in 2003.[15] Had this not occurred, today's cars would be an estimated 33 percent more fuel-efficient than current levels. Attempts that were made in the last decade to render automobiles more fuel-efficient were offset by North Americans' attachment to large vehicles.

Car-dependent suburban developments have radically altered

places. Natural and agricultural landscapes were built and paved over to create what James Howard Kunstler called "the Geography of Nowhere".[16] The vibrant community that in older towns took centuries to evolve, the graceful aging necessary to create a sense of real place, where residents, businesses, and institutions mix, did not materialize in suburbia. Low residential density cannot sustain neighborhood convenience stores, bookstores, and cafés because of the lack of economy of scale.

How can we turn things around? Can we retool or alter existing suburban communities? Can we plan new ones differently so they become denser and more livable? Will we be willing to give up spaciousness and, as a result, alter our lifestyles?

Current suburban densities of 4 to 7 dwelling units per acre (10 to 17 dwelling units per hectare) need to be augmented to at least 15 to 35 dwelling units per acre (37 to 86 units per hectare), to create active and vibrant places. With the diminishing size of the average North American household, it is likely that higher densities than these will be needed in the future. Also, as our population becomes demographically more diverse and the proportion of singles, single-parent families, childless couples, and the elderly increases, creating communities with mixed housing types will make greater economic and social sense. Small businesses such as cafés, bookstores, dental clinics, and home offices may find themselves in the heart of communities again.

To increase the density of existing neighborhoods, lower floors or basements can be made into self-contained units and rented out. Free-standing structures known as garden suites or granny flats can be constructed at the rear of new or existing homes for extended family living. When a single-story structure is demolished it can be replaced by a two-story house, although not by a "monster home", with little effect on streetscape. We may want to reconsider building heights, which were set at 35 feet (10.7 meters)—the tallest spot that a fireman's ladder could reach—many decades ago. An additional 5 feet (1.5 meters) and a different roof angle will enable homeowners to have expanded living space in an attic.

If we are to make more room for housing, oversized roads need to be reduced from their current 60-foot (18-meter) right-of-way. This width was the radius needed by a carriage drawn by four horses to make a 360-degree turn. Parking needs to be rethought. Moving garages from their current location on the side or front of dwellings to the rear, served by a lane, will result in narrower lots.

The desire to limit sprawl and recreate the sense of place we find in old towns is at the heart of the Neo-Traditional Development Movement which began in the United States in the 1980s. The planning of new communities, such as Seaside, Florida, includes narrow streets, pedestrian networks, civic squares, and less visible parking places.

An old city which possesses these qualities and which has aged beautifully is Savannah, Georgia, where Spanish moss hangs from lush green oak trees that line streets and fill squares framed by a blend of lavish mansions, townhouses, apartment buildings, stores, and restaurants.

The land on which Savannah now exists was settled in 1733 by a group of a hundred and fourteen British colonists led by James Oglethorpe. The settlers chose a flat piece of land some 10 miles (16 kilometers) from the sea on which to build a city. Oglethorpe, historians suggest, modeled Savannah after traditional Roman military camps as well as English town-planning principles of the time. Whatever the source of the plan, its small footprint made it easy to defend.[17]

It was based on a system of wards made up of narrow lots with open public spaces at their center. Despite its high density, it does not feel cramped since the squares' proportions are on a comfortable human scale. Beautifully landscaped, each square has a different middle feature. Some have statues of governors and generals from the Civil War era when the town was the South's capital, and others have bandstands painted white. Savannah was designed when carriages roamed the streets and it has no visible garages. Instead, back lanes and roadsides are used for cars. Short setbacks relate the homes beautifully to the street and a sliver of green in front of each house makes walking on the nearby sidewalk pleasant. Stairs, designed parallel to sidewalks, lead pedestrians to the first-floor entries of townhouses and apartments.[17]

Over the years the homes have been transformed. Some mansions have been turned into multifamily dwellings. Floors have been added and commercial premises have been introduced in others, while respecting the buildings' original character. There are institutional, religious, and commercial buildings in Savannah. Most noticeable is the Cotton Exchange building on the bank of the Savannah River; it has an upper street-level entrance and an entrance facing a lower river promenade where restaurants with outdoor seating now exist.

It makes one wonder, however, why we can't learn from the common sense visible in places like Savannah, which has organically evolved over centuries and is still functioning well. Higher densities, when properly implemented, can foster livable communities where people contribute to and enjoy a real sense of place. The question remains: will people be willing to trade off large backyards and wide roads for livability? Many, I guess, will not. Others, municipal leaders among them, will realize that sprawl has an environmental, social, and economic toll, and the time for a U-turn has arrived.

Four

Turnips in Dalian

DALIAN WAS WAKING UP. From the window of my room on the seventeenth floor of Hotel Furama, I could see night being switched off as a red glow kindled the sunrise over the horizon. In the port just in front, huge cranes began their slow and determined movement, hauling orange containers onto a large ship. In the distance, skyscrapers whose heads were engulfed in morning mist began to be revealed like paper cutouts.

I came to Dalian to participate in a United Nations-sponsored conference that coincided with the fiftieth anniversary of the founding of the People's Republic of China. The city is in transition between its agrarian past and a technological future. It is one of China's designated development zones. Flags draped the streets and huge images of former and present leaders smiled and waved from billboards.

It was 5 a.m. and I was up. Meetings weren't to begin until much later. I decided to head down into the streets that had begun returning to life.

From Renmin Road, Dalian's main thoroughfare, I ventured into a side street. Reaching into my pocket, I realized that I had left my city map in the hotel. I decided to carry on without it. I offered a greeting to a merchant who was unlocking a metal shutter. He returned my smile, probably wondering what a foreigner was doing out so early. Dumplings in a steaming soup were for sale at a corner stand; two patrons sat on metal cans and ate.

I walked to the next corner where I noticed a commotion of loaded pushcarts and people entering and exiting a yard. I followed them and found myself in a market framed by traditional four-story, shabby-looking buildings. It was a unique sight with sounds and smells that stood in marked contrast to the barren streets that I had just crossed.

Produce and other goods were arranged in parallel lines on the ground, in no apparent order. Vendors—peasants, it seemed, who farmed in the area, and other traders—sold to urban dwellers who resided nearby. Celery, turnips, green onions, and leeks looked freshly harvested. Buyers, holding cotton bags, pointed, asked for a price, and, at times, bargained. The seller grabbed the item and placed it on a handheld scale. Money was exchanged. Fried food and dumplings were cooked and sold in a corner. Sea creatures were tucked in between fruit and vegetables. Unshaven, tired-looking fishermen snatched handfuls of crabs and shrimp, shoved them into folded newspaper, and handed them over to customers. There were also household goods for sale: pots and pans, can openers, knives, screwdrivers, undergarments, socks.

I advanced slowly from vendor to vendor, politely rebuffing soliciting gestures, signaling that I was only looking. It was a true feast for the senses.

"What makes this market different?" I wondered. Was it the raw quality of the place: a mercantile act stripped of the trappings that we Westerners are used to? There were no plastic bags, price tags, or uniformed salespeople. Was it the direct exchange between farmer and consumer? Perhaps it was the produce, some of which I did not recognize, and the feeling of being a jetlagged foreigner in an unexpected spot at dawn. I was experiencing a sense of place that brought me closer to the culinary culture of people who minutes ago were total strangers. I could sense their story and felt I could know who they were.

I like to visit markets. I grew up on the edge of one; as a child I frequented Tel Aviv's Shuk Ha'Carmel with its main street and alleys. My head barely reaching the stalls' countertops, I helped my mother carry bags home on Fridays after school. I recall the verses that vendors cried out to promote sweet grapes and juicy tomatoes.

Neatly arranged rows of cow tongues, piles of chicken livers, and fish laced with crushed ice were displayed in the storefronts.

My voyages have taken me to other markets. I have sunk my bare palm into a bag of white beans in Istanbul's Spice Bazaar, listened to birds in Hong Kong's Bird Market, and watched merchants throwing fish to one another in Seattle's Public Market. I have toured daily, weekly, and monthly markets in small and large towns. But what I treasure most are the markets in the hearts of urban neighborhoods, authentic old markets that have become features of their surroundings, where vendors may know their patron's names and choices, and where generosity of spirit seems more important than neatness.

Markets have become a casualty of modern planning, however. Short-sightedness has chased a prime social and economic institution out of our communities. How did that happen?

To understand their evolution, one needs to recall the development of agriculture and trade and follow a thread that goes back to a time when most societies were made up of hunters and gatherers and survived on what nature could provide. People lived in bands whose size was determined by food supply. It is estimated that an area of 4,500 to 320,000 acres (1,800 to 130,000 hectares) per person was required to maintain an early settlement.[1] This pattern was transformed with the discovery of agriculture. Bands still relied on their hunting and gathering skills, but when animals were domesticated, seeds planted, and crops harvested, there was sufficient food for the farmer's household, and leftovers for trade. The food supply chain no longer decided the group's size, which rapidly expanded.

The skills needed in permanent settlements were diverse. Some specialized in tool-making, others in erecting homes, for example, and there were those—the majority, perhaps—who grew and harvested food. Societies re-arranged themselves and trading food for commodities or services became common. In later centuries, as communities grew in size, commerce became more important and formalized in location and process. Weekly days were chosen for buying and selling livestock and other commodities, an activity

named "market", *mercatus* in Latin, which means the activity of
trading, dealing, or buying as well as the marketplace where these
activities occur.[2] The name was common in Europe, in particular
in settlements with Roman origins. The word "bazaar" has Persian
roots and was used in Turkey, and the word *souq* was common in
the Arab world. Along with the evolution of commerce and the
invention of currencies, the physical forms of markets varied and
progressed.

In Europe, between the tenth and eleventh centuries, the activity
of exchanging goods and money usually settled just outside the
initial residential nucleus, near a gate, an important communication
route, or the city walls.[3] In towns endowed with waterways, markets
were established on or near a riverbank, like the one on the River
Seine in Paris. In places that had access to the sea, markets develop
near the water, like the one in Venice that flourished in the Rialto
district. They became the sites of noisy retail markets as well as
silent exchanges.

Other markets, primarily those built in Roman towns, emerged
at the intersection of two major urban arteries perpendicular to
each other, the *cardo maximus* and *decumanus maximus*. Stores
along the Cardo are still visible in Jerusalem's Old City, where merchants had their businesses and residences. The creation of a market
square at the intersection of the two main streets took place in
Florence in 1303 as the Commune, the city's governing body,
acquired and demolished the Nerli house.[4]

Markets adopted different operational forms, depending on
the community's size and the culture of trade. They could be held
daily, weekly, or even monthly. The less frequent markets resembled
today's agricultural fairs, to which peasants and traders come from
afar. Farmer's markets, primarily in small communities where
seasonal produce was sold, consisted of a simple display of goods
on the ground. It was a short-term engagement, hours or days, much
like the one I saw in Dalian. When trading evolved and the
institution of middleman flourished, commerce and the place of
business changed as well. Growers no longer needed to travel to

markets, but traded with merchants who then sold to the public. The vendors needed stalls for storage and display and, of course, they needed a flow of customers. Such, for example, is the market at St. Albans, a small town near London, England. It began to operate in the tenth century, has changed little, and still welcomes the public every Wednesday and Saturday.

There was always a tendency for vendors of similar goods to locate their stalls near each other because it was easier for merchants to draw patrons to their sections and for buyers to find items and compare prices when similar products were in proximity to each other. In larger towns, there were enough vendors of the same type of product to constitute their own market. Fish markets were located near the harbor, where fishermen could easily display their daily catch. Meat, fruits, vegetables, flowers, clothing—markets evolved for many types of goods.

With the expansion of cities came the realization that markets were valuable sources of tax revenue. Formal covered structures replaced ramshackle stalls as municipal governments saw the advantages of being able to better maintain hygiene. Istanbul's Grand Bazaar was such a place. It has been operating since the mid-fifteenth century. The building stretches over 74 acres (30 hectares); it houses hundreds of shops and thousands of tradesmen in dozens of streets, alleys, and courtyards. It has many specialty areas, the goldsmiths, for example, as well as areas for clothing, footwear, leather and hides, furniture, and many other goods.[5] A short distance away, one finds the Spice Bazaar, a seventeenth-century L-shaped structure with leaded domes and some eighty shops. Also known as the Egyptian Bazaar, it was a trading post for Middle Eastern and European merchants. In addition to spices, cheese, dried meat, jam, nuts, and soap are sold by merchants who congregate in their own spots.

Stores in bustling markets were often the site of manufacturing. Goods were produced in the rear, to be sold at a front counter or a window. Markets had a secondary, somewhat hidden, layer of commerce, made up of those who cared for and benefited from the merchants and their clients. Mobile peddlers, often children, carried their goods on their backs, heads or pushcarts. To this day, the sight of a man carrying a large bronze vessel, selling *tamarhindy*, a cold drink made of dates, is common in Middle Eastern markets.

Markets played a significant role in the development of local economies, and they contributed to the social fabric of a community. The development of monetary systems enabled farmers to receive currency rather than barter for goods or services. The hub of business was the market; subsidiary financial institutions became formalized in the Middle Ages. Banking and lending establishments offered loans to those who wished to initiate an enterprise. They were catalysts to a thriving local economy. With the formal establishment of mints, each region had its own currency and a defined geographic limit for taxing and trading. Merchants began to pay duties to be awarded the right to trade by local authorities. Certain locations on main market streets were more valuable in attracting customers, and therefore commanded higher taxes.

The contribution of the market to the social fabric of its communities was significant. In addition to being a place of trade, it was a meeting point. Vendors knew their regular clients' names and buying habits. Shoppers, some of whom frequented the market daily, encountered their friends, neighbors, and acquaintances and exchanged information.[6] Social institutions such as pubs and inns thrived near the market. Merchants who traveled from afar could stay overnight before heading back home. Shoppers could prolong their stay to hear the latest political news or exchange gossip. Vendors could meet each other after hours to discuss business matters and each others' lives. There were emotional ties and mutual support among vendors who, at times, formed collectives to ensure that pricing limits would be maintained. There was a familiarity and loyalty between vendors and shoppers, which promoted an ethic of quality products and honest exchange.

People of all ages and a range of social classes mixed in the market. It was the hub of information exchange, the forerunner of today's print and electronic media. Public announcements were made in the nearby square, and posters displayed. Being in the market was entertaining. You could hear people bargain and marvel at the theatrical skills of the vendors and their ability to stimulate conversation and display their goods in pleasing and attractive ways.[6]

The development of North American markets benefited from the trading experience that European settlers brought with them. New arrivals were familiar with monetary systems and trading practices and had urban know-how. Streets crowded with makeshift stalls in neighborhoods populated by immigrants in cities like New York or Chicago were common well into the twentieth century.

Public markets thrived in Europe and North America. They derived from the market buildings of earlier centuries, but more attention was paid in their design to considerations of function and appearance. In most cities, the public market was centrally located, a massive building with easily distinguished architecture.

In her book *Public Markets and Civic Culture*, Helen Tangires suggests that "[t]he public market is a key piece in understanding the profoundly important shift from agrarian to industrial food systems in nineteenth-century America." She says that, more than a place to buy and sell food, public markets were civic spaces, the common ground "where citizens and governments defined the shared values of the community." Public markets were places where the "moral economy" was exercised, where unwritten codes of cleanliness, freshness, and, above all, affordable pricing, were carefully adhered to.[7]

Market architects aimed to create safe and attractive buildings that would draw bourgeois consumers. Whereas earlier markets had been rough-and-ready places from which the upper classes, particularly women, stayed away, public markets offered an appealing environment, with tiled floors and walls, lots of space to move around, and attractive well-lit vending counters. Their design promoted civility, friendliness, and respect.

Food growing and trade evolved in the aftermath of the Industrial Revolution. Mechanization enabled large-scale production with fewer helping hands. Agricultural produce could be brought to market rapidly by railway. Greater variety from afar and larger quantities were sold at lower prices. There was a boom in the construction of public markets. In 1870, some sixty-six new public markets were constructed in England—11 percent of all the new markets that were built during the century.[7] Construction of markets also accelerated in North American cities around that time.

The architecture of public markets evolved. The desire to free space from columns, to build on several levels, and to let in natural light, led to the use of steel and glass architecture, which had advanced with the development of railway stations and exhibition halls. Prefabricated cast iron structures with large windows, often encased in a brick envelope, were the hallmark of European and North American markets, such as Barcelona's Mercat de la Boqueria or Chicago's Central Market.

With rapid urbanization and the emergence of the sprawling metropolis, larger quantities of food had to reach cities. Daily direct supply by growers to large and small markets with many stalls was cumbersome. This led to the development of wholesale terminal markets—a single structure or series of buildings designed for storage and distribution of produce, like the Bronx Terminal Market in New York City. They were linked to railways, highways, and waterways. Food was stored there, often refrigerated, before it was distributed regionally. It became common for vendors in small markets and shops to buy directly from wholesalers whom they visited daily. The gap between the growers and consumers increased.

Most of the many suburbs developed after World War II were located on former farmland, which had supplied the food that cities consumed. Produce now had to come from farther away by truck or train. With a decline in the population density in the core of many cities, public markets had fewer patrons. Suburbanites needed their own places to buy food. Enter the supermarket.

Suitably named in Hollywood during the 1930s, two types of supermarkets emerged. The first emphasized style. The other markets specialized in lower prices and larger volume. They were initiated by independent merchants who wanted to challenge the dominance of food retailers who sold to grocery stores. They sold for cash, provided no delivery services, and filled their stores with nationally-branded and advertised products.[8]

In 1935, there were about three hundred supermarkets in the United States, a figure that mushroomed to 6,175 by 1940. In 1936, A&P operated twenty supermarkets and by 1941, it had opened 1,594. As the population of city centers declined, A&P began to close its urban outlets, which dropped from around fifteen thousand in the mid-1930s to about six thousand by the early 1940s.[8]

Supermarkets dealt city markets a major blow. Food-buying habits were changing in the suburbs. Freshness of food and shopping habits that promoted a close-knit social fabric were traded for convenience and cordial, if superficial, human relationships. On weekends, busy householders drove to a food store to stock up for the week. Eventually, some supermarkets began to disguise themselves as markets by changing the way produce was displayed or even dressing employees in period clothing. They began to prepare cooked food on-site. There were mini fish and meat markets and bakeries fragrant with the smell of fresh bread, all under one roof along with aisles full of canned food and other household goods.

Agricultural production changed as family-run farms were replaced by large industrial operations that supplied food processors and wholesalers. Direct exchange between farmers or vendors and citizens in markets, which for centuries contributed to making places livable, all but disappeared.

Food consumption habits changed. Households gradually shifted to ready-to-serve convenience food. In 2004, a *Newsweek* article reported that only a third of all dinner entrées were entirely homemade; fully 47 percent of all suppers eaten at home did not involve turning on the stove at all, and the area in supermarkets dedicated to selling prepared dinners has increased by 168 percent since 1993.[9] Few peel tomatoes to make Grandma's lasagna and even that American icon, the burger, is sold frozen in a bun with condiments. Once-a-week shopping for convenient, ready-to-serve food has led to expanded cupboard space and larger refrigerators and many households have added a separate freezer in the basement for long-term storage. Meanwhile, the real kitchens where food is actually prepared have in many cases moved to efficient plants somewhere in the industrial part of town.

Yet, it seems that the natural instincts of the buying public have served it well when it has come to saving vital commercial and social institutions, such as old-style markets, from complete extinction. The quest for freshness, lower prices, and direct exchange with the grower led to a resurgence of farmers' markets, which are generally recurring at fixed locations where products are sold by the farmers themselves. In the U.S., for example, there were about 340 farmers' markets in 1970, and over three thousand in 2001.[1] Some are located in structures to which food producers drive, and are open daily. Others operate during summer and autumn months. They may be less formal and products are sold from the back of trucks or makeshift stalls.

Studies show that growers are inclined to sell in farmers' markets because they often see them as the best, or the most profitable, venue for selling their produce. Consumers visit them because they provide high quality produce at a reasonable price.[11] In a survey of reasons for shopping in farmers' markets, 63 percent of the respondants answered that freshness was their prime reason. Fifty-four percent indicated price savings, and the social atmosphere drew 12 percent.[12] Market gardeners and other small-scale farmers, many of whom farm part-time, drive, on average, 19 miles (30 kilometers) to their place of trade. Their customers come primarily from neighborhoods adjacent to the market; once again, markets have begun to play an important social role by creating a local public meeting point. Their contribution to local economies is of high value, as they lead to spending in nearby shops, which generates further tax revenue. Some analysts suggest that farmers' markets create jobs, build new businesses, strengthen and diversify regional agriculture, and elevate farm profitability.[13] Granville Island Market in Vancouver created 3.2 full-time and 4.3 part-time jobs per vendor, for example. Markets have become a tourist draw for out-of-the-region visitors. In Syracuse, New York, the Dutin Farmers' Market has been the catalyst for many city programs in the downtown area, with free bus touring on market days, and the turning of several streets into pedestrian malls where local artists display their work.[14]

The increased popularity of farmers' markets contributes to communities' sustainability. Local growers are supported. Food does not travel from afar and emission levels are reduced. Produce that is to be sold direct by the grower does not have to be chemically treated to increase its shelf life, which improves overall public health.[15]

Urban environments are made up of land uses whose primary function is to support basic human needs. We build homes to shelter people and factories for them to work in. There are, however, places that play a dual role. They not only provide basic amenities and contribute to economic vitality, but they act as social magnets. Markets are such places. They are scenes of trade, as well as places for communal interaction and gathering spots where one can watch the theatre of life. As I walked away from the morning market I'd stumbled onto in Dalian, I realized that our communal fabric can only be enriched by their existence. We should keep them vibrant.

Five

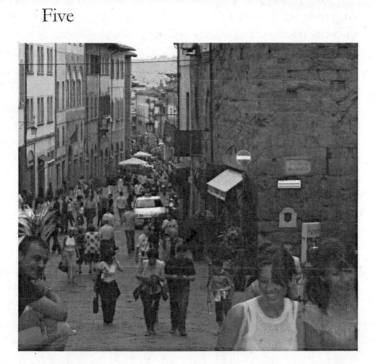

Hugging in Casole d'Elsa

I went to Casole d'Elsa, 22 miles (35 kilometers) west of Siena on the advice of my Tuscan host. I was looking for someplace quaint, a small place, less frequented by tourists. The curved road to Casole was busy. Many locals were headed in my direction, to judge by the licence plates on the cars around me. Their passengers appeared to be having animated conversations. In the distance I could see buildings clustered on a hilltop.

A man was directing traffic towards an improvised parking lot. I parked and walked uphill, surrounded by people in a festive mood. Nicely dressed men and women hugged and kissed, teenagers yelled, and children chased each other.

As I turned a corner, I saw people standing next to two freshly-painted white picket fences. A 20-foot (6-meter) path lay between them. It curved and disappeared around the hillside. Colorful flags bearing crests were affixed intermittently to poles, and many people carried flags. I could hear, and understand with my rudimentary Italian, the word "*cavalli*" ("horses") and realized that my good fortune had brought me to a place where a horse race was about to commence. People were discussing riders, their horses, and the contest's outcome. Some spectators leaned on the fence while others, mostly seniors who seemed to know each other well, sat on stools, waiting.

Il Palio has taken place in Casole on the second Sunday in July since the seventeenth century. Each of the town's wards, the *contradas*, designates a horse and jockey.

The *contrada*, a defined administrative district, has a history rooted in age-old military campaigns when men were called to defend a city-state against invaders. The *contradas* have few powers today, but their members are bound by traditions and family ties. Each ward has a flag and there are distinctive songs that are sung at marriages and funerals.

From afar I heard a loud roar. Everyone stood up. People craned their necks and toddlers on their parents' shoulders pointed. A pack of riders appeared over the horizon, approached fast, and galloped past in a whoosh.

I happened to be surrounded by residents of the winning *contrada*, Pievalle. "Donatini! Donatini!" they yelled, as they hailed the rider. To my surprise, an overjoyed old man hugged me. A short while ago, I had been a total stranger, a visitor from afar. Now I felt I was part of their celebration. The spectators began a post-race analysis. I found myself eagerly listening.

The sun was setting as I worked my way through the dispersing spectators. They continued waving their flags, and engaged in impassioned discussions of the race, accompanied by hand gestures. This was a joyous scene, with a certain authenticity.

I climbed a steep set of stairs and arrived at the main square. Here was La Rocca, the town hall. I watched the thick crowd dividing along narrow streets into their *contradas*. Flags moved gently in the evening breeze. They were attached to guardrails in front of the windows. Flowers in ceramic pots cascaded from the sills.

Casole d'Elsa was just the place I was looking for! Small, shy, simple, with cobblestone roads and storefronts with modest signs on the ground level of two-story stone buildings, just the bare essentials tucked into each other, nicely.

It was growing dark as I wandered through the town. People congregated in restaurants and sat at tables in courtyards and small squares. They were talking, making signs to each other, kissing. Toasts were drunk with wine. I admired, and even envied, what I saw. I wondered whether this outpouring of camaraderie can only happen in places with long-standing traditions, among people whose roots are embedded in the locale. Did Casole have something in its physical make-up, perhaps, that contributed to such relationships? I believe it did. The dense, tiny town, with its narrow streets and attached buildings, offered a backdrop for socializing. "Why don't contemporary North American neighborhoods look and feel like Casole?" I wondered. How does urban design affect human relations? Is proper urban design vital to the creation of sense of place?

Many things affect behavior, of course, and only some are affected by the "place". Culture and social trends also shape who we are. Western societies have undergone a transition in recent decades. In the past, the individual was part of a well-crafted social fabric, but this has unraveled and left a noticeable mark on our neighborhoods.

In the past half century, not only have we planned developments with lower densities, but also fewer people reside in each home. Our demographic composition has changed with the decline of what demographers tag "traditional households". Married couples with children now make up less than one-quarter of all households, a significant drop from about one-half in 1960. There has been an increase in the number of those who remain single; they constitute a quarter of North America's adult population. Single-parent families account for 10 percent of households. With these trends, fewer people are stepping out of front doors—not a good recipe for a chance encounter on a local street.

A family type which I spotted in Casole, and which has nearly vanished from our social tapestry, is the extended family. Now it is rare in North America for several generations to occupy a home. It is unusual to spot a grandparent and a grandchild, who reside in the same dwelling, stepping out for a stroll. The old live further away, most likely with other old folks. Our places of living are becoming demographically monolithic, made up of very similar households of the same age and wealth group. The ancestors of the crowd with which I rubbed shoulders in Tuscany were born and raised there. Intra-marriage has bonded clans to form common histories and blood relationships. If someone encountered an acquaintance on the street, he or she not only knew where the person lived, but they could draw in their mind a family tree to which that person belonged and to which they were, perhaps, be related. In North America, the transitory nature of contemporary society and of our residency has affected our interaction. Not many people plant deep roots in their chosen neighborhoods.

Not surprisingly, home buyers give primary consideration to the resale value of their house. Studies show that renters will buy homes in neighborhoods with urban and social characteristics that are likely to satisfy their own desires and those of future buyers of their homes.[1] People buy with the hope that upward mobility and the opportunity for a bigger and better place may be around the corner. The home is regarded as an asset that may be liquidated and, along with it, the social network that was formed during the residency, to be perhaps kept in a computer database. North Americans move on average every five years. We tend to see more unrecognizable faces on our streets than we used to because the neighbors keep changing.

Along with Western society's demographic transformation have come lifestyle changes. Manners, attitudes and habits have affected relationships. We spend more time indoors than we used to. Studies demonstrate that time devoted to meaningful interactions between family members at home has been reduced. Our preoccupation with electronic media and the endless rush to catch up with work or chores leaves little time for quality conversations or family activities.[5]

The time spent in front of information appliances at home has grown. In 2002, the average hours of television-viewing per week for Canadians aged 12 and over was 21.8.[2] Now in the age of social media like Facebook, face-to-face conversations have been replaced by cyber-communication. We do not chat with neighbors at the grocery store checkouts because groceries can now be ordered online and delivered to our doorstep. A walk to a local post office to mail a letter has been replaced by pressing an e-mail send command. The magnitude of these demographic and lifestyle changes is reflected in changes to our urban landscape, chief among them, our streets.

Since the invention of the car and its proliferation, local road systems have expanded consistently and considerably. It seems, at times, that houses are an afterthought of street design, which can occupy some 30 percent to 50 percent of the total area under development. In America's first planned suburbs of the 1920s, streets measured 18 feet (5.5 meters) wide. When most suburban zoning laws were enacted in the 1950s, fire marshals were mandated to verify that a 40-foot-(12-meter) long fire engine could access every house and make a U-turn on every street, despite the fact that the homes were situated on loop roads and fire hydrants were placed every 1,000 feet (300 meters). Designing shorter trucks apparently did not enter anyone's mind.[3]

In many communities, municipal planning bylaws set new houses back a minimum of 20 feet (6 meters) and in some case even 30 feet (9 meters) from the lot line, further eroding intimacy. One of the principal reasons for the setback was the questionable notion that a wide boulevard made the street look more distinguished. The other reason was access to garages, which had become a central preoccupation of car-dependent municipalities, developers, and home buyers. It also allowed drivers to park their cars outdoors in front of their dwelling. On suburban streets there are often no pedestrians. Stopping for a conversation with an acquaintance on a barren sidewalk, if there is one, does not feel the same as in a city core. What in older homes was a cosy living room, has become a room the size of a dance hall.

Home design on a human scale further eroded when more family members began to own cars and needed places to house them all indoors. Garages with double and sometimes triple doors have begun to dominate the built landscape in new suburbs. Sometimes you have to search for the main door. It seems houses look like car washes. Since some municipalities have mandated up to four parking spots per home, garages have to be located at the front of the house. It is the only place where so many cars will fit. Ironically, garages have become huge closets for unused household goods. Garden chairs, lawn mowers, bicycles, suitcases, and other items are stored there, while the cars are parked in the driveway or on the street.

Affixing garages to the front of houses has meant that no trees could be planted along the wide, paved driveway. A road with a row of homes with such driveways is probably treeless, with the loss of atmosphere that that entails. There are no shady spots to stand and chat with neighbors. Placing garages up front has resulted in another indirect social toll: in many cases there are no more front porches, and often not even a window.

Porches, verandas, or stoops actually play an important role in fostering community relations. In *Geography of Home*, Akiko Busch writes, "Halfway inside the house and halfway outside, the very ambiguity of the front porch or stoop has encouraged a variety of interpretations and uses over the years." The front porch's social function was as important as its architectural definitions.[4] The front porch has acted as a sort of exterior living room that, when built broad and deep, enables occupants to entertain guests and enjoy cool summer breezes. The informality of the space did not oblige the owner to invite guests in, yet they were still being received in the owner's domain. They offered visual contact with neighbors or strangers who were passing by, and the opportunity to nod, wave, or start a conversation. The front porch was more than an external design artefact, a "mad room" as it was called in New England. It helped people who shared the street maintain eye contact, cement existing relationships, begin new ones, and guard each other's property.

Realizing that fewer people were walking, some municipalities decided that new housing developments could do without sidewalks altogether. That sliver of paved area on one or both sides of the road was now added to the street itself. In some cases, a narrow concrete pad 18 inches (46 centimeters) wide, with a curb, was left to mark the edge of the road. Walking in these suburban developments has become a risky affair, requiring people to watch for approaching cars. Parents pushing strollers or seniors have been gradually discouraged from venturing out for a walk.

Pedestrian paths let people traverse neighborhoods safely, but they rarely exist nowadays. In cities, alleys or lanes created a secondary commuting network. Alleyways—utilitarian but also the place where kids played, deliveries were made, and trash was collected—all but disappeared with the birth of suburban land subdivision. Some municipalities regarded them as unsafe or requiring maintenance. Developers realized that they could add that rear strip of land to each house, making a big backyard even bigger, and suburban homeowners didn't mind having larger yards. Paths between homes have largely been squeezed out of master plans as well, once again, in the name of safety and land efficiency. Adults and children who wanted to take a short walk and pay a visit to a friend's home just behind them lost another comfortable route and either had to walk on a sidewalk-less street, drive, or be driven.

Once the sidewalk disappeared, street benches fell by the wayside, as there was hardly a place left to place them. Benches were gestures of kindness, a mark of civility on which an elderly person could sit, a jogger rest, and a reader enjoy a book on a sunny day while waiting for a bus, perhaps beginning a conversation with whomever was sitting beside him. Street corners were places where community announcements were posted and next to which people would congregate to read what was happening. Notice boards, common street furniture in older times, faded away from our streets, to be recently replaced by electronic messaging.

Are relationships among the people who inhabit a community necessary to foster a sense of place? They certainly are. Sense of place is an outcome of the physical features that surround us, such as roads and buildings and the spaces in between, and of the interactions that happen among those for whom the places were built. It is a stretch to think that proper planning and urban design can foster improved human relations, but what they can do is offer opportunities for such relations to occur.

Six

Swings in Petach Tikva

NEAR THE STOP WHERE I GOT OFF THE BUS, I saw a man with a round face and thinning yellow hair leaning on a second-floor balcony guardrail. I decided to walk closer and ask him. I could not tell his age, forty perhaps, maybe forty-five. He faced the sun, smoked, and looked away. I called out to draw his attention. He turned and noticed me.

"Do you know the Lev family, who lived in this building?" I asked.

"Who are you?" he wanted to know.

"I lived right under them in the 1950s," I said.

"Let me come down," he offered. Moments later, he met me on the sidewalk. We faced each other, his head barely reaching my shoulder height.

"I am Lev, Shalom Lev," he said. I introduced myself and we shook hands. We remembered each other from childhood. I told him that I lived in Canada now, and that I had come to see what had happened to my childhood place. I asked him about old friends; he knew some, but had lost contact with most. "The neighborhood has changed a lot," he said.

We began a slow stroll along the narrow, treed street that circled my old home. Shalom pointed to some of the apartments in which friends had lived and tried to recall where they were now. We arrived at a park where Shalom, his two younger brothers, other kids from the surrounding fourplexes, and I had passed time together. I spotted my bedroom window from where I stood. In those long-ago afternoons, as the first of my friends arrived to play, he would call for me. I'd ask my mother's permission and join them.

The park had not changed much. A small patch, some 350 feet by 100 feet (100 meters by 30 meters), it was part of a subdivision—a *shikun*—on the edge of a small Israeli town called Petach Tikva, which had been constructed to house new immigrants like my parents. The white stucco fronts of most of the buildings faced the park, with front pathways extending to it. Parents could easily watch their children from the balconies. I recalled the sound of rotating sprinklers on a hot summer evening, the smell of freshly cut grass, and my father calling me to come home for dinner.

The unpaved center was made for play. I remembered the many games and the sound of shouting children chasing each other. There was a seesaw, swing, "carousel"—a rotating, round set of benches—for older kids and a sandbox full of toddlers. Benches were placed under trees along the perimeter, where people could sit to watch the children and have animated conversations with each other. It was safe, naïve, much like the rest of our new community, with its nearby school, four-shop strip, and medical clinic.

At the far end of the park I noticed Gan Dina, my single-story daycare with its red tile roof. What a clever idea it was, I thought, to place a daycare near a park where we could play under the watchful eye of a teacher.

I have fond memories of the short, slow walk home at the day's end. There was a lot of common sense in the planning of my childhood place: family homes edging a park with narrow streets to slow traffic and pathways on which kids and adults with toddlers could walk in safety. As I rode my nostalgic rollercoaster that morning, reminiscing of times long past and reflecting on faded images, I realized that many of my memories were associated with playing outdoors. I wondered why this park was etched in my mind at all, and why compact play spaces have been excluded from the planning of many new residential developments. What happened to play, and more so, to playgrounds? Has the joy of being, and playing, outside, been replaced by competing indoor interests? Will it affect children's development and their road to adulthood?

The instinct of children to explore the world through play dates back centuries. There are vague references to informal play areas throughout urban history. Essentially, they were part of an open space system, a specialized one, in cities. In classical Greek planning, there were two recognized open spaces in every town. The better known of the two was the *agora*, a centrally located gathering space and the hub of trade. The other place was the *Plaleia*, in which community and personal celebration happened. Children played, unsupervised, in both.[1] In later eras, there were other public places which doubled as locations for children's play. A serious recognition for the need for formal play areas and playgrounds came, however, only after 1870.[2]

Until then, children were not thought of as individuals different from adults. Historian J. H. Plumb suggests that today's conception of a children's world with "fairy tale stories, games, toys, special books for learning, even the idea of childhood itself is a European invention of the past four hundred years."[3] Earlier, their world was not separated from that of an adult. They took part in providing for their families through hard work and, when allowed free time to play, it likely occurred in public spaces, at least in urban areas.[1] In the aftermath of the Industrial Revolution, social reformers began to include the welfare of children among their concerns. Mandatory schooling was a chief recognition that childhood is a separate domain from adulthood, and formal education was made part of growing up.

The scientific investigation of children's intellectual skills was first undertaken in the mid-nineteenth century. Scholars who studied childhood development, such as Friedrich Froebel, Maria Montessori, Jean Piaget, and Susan Isaacs agree that healthy growth, including physical, emotional, social, and intellectual aspects, is based on stimulating learning experiences that arouse the learner's interest. They recognized that play is an area where children's natural curiosity guides their learning. In her book *Playground Design*, Anse Eriksen suggests that the new notion was that "[t]hrough play, they may develop a sense of security, confidence and safety, a feeling of

being loved, strong relationships with others and a sense of indepen-
dence and of initiative."[1]

It was demonstrated that lack of such stimulation at an early
age can negatively affect children's transition into adulthood. Growing up in boring environments, and having only unchallenging
experiences, can be harmful to development.

Researchers have suggested that play offers a variety of stimu-
lations that parallel development. Physical stimuli relate to sensory
and motor skills and include being touched, seeing colors, or hearing
sounds, among others. Motor activities include hand-eye and eye-
foot coordination; they are developed through running, climbing,
and crawling, for example. Perceptual stimulation helps children
develop the ability to recognize patterns such as familiar streets or
repetition of sounds and music. Emotional stimulation is recognized as essential to improve a child's ability to deal with difficult
or stressful situations in childhood and later. Social stimulation
allows a child to try on self-images, connect with peers, and develop
human relationships. Intellectual stimulation is vital to the
development of the mind. It comes through exploring, working
alone, communicating, fantasizing, and having novel experiences.[4]

The studies on child development attracted attention and pro-
voked action in the design of play spaces. In 1837, Friedrich Froebel,
an educator, proposed the kindergarten, a garden for children based
on the premise that play areas should mimic country life of which
children were deprived in the crowded, polluted cities.[5] Specialized
play equipment was invented around the same time. Swings, rocking
horses, and bicycles made their appearance during the Victorian
era and were installed in selected public, but mostly private,
domains.[6]

The introduction of North America's first freestanding, pur-
pose-built playgrounds in the 1880s had an ulterior motive.
According to Dominick Cavallo in *Muscles and Morals*, urban
reformers believed that "supervised team play for male adolescents
organized by social workers on municipal playgrounds would
insulate youngsters from the pervasive city vices, act as a deterrent

against juvenile crime, and provide them with supervision and moral purpose missing from their lives."[7] It was seen as a way to integrate immigrant children into society and instill in them true American values. Playgrounds, some believed, could become a melting pot of sorts, bringing together kids of different heritages.

Most of the first planned playgrounds were initiated by private philanthropic organizations. They became features of major American cities around the turn of the nineteenth century. Built in dense neighborhoods, they had sandboxes, an idea imported from Germany. Swings and seesaws were placed on hard surfaces that were enclosed by tall fences. The Charles Bank Playground in Boston is an example. It was designed by Frederick Law Olmsted and had an open air gymnasium with a running track and a well-equipped play area.

The founding in 1906 of the Playground Association of America (PAA) was an important step in the development of play spaces. Municipal authorities began to assume responsibility for the welfare of children within their boundaries.

An additional milestone was the incorporation of playtime and physical exercise into the school curriculum, which was introduced in Gary, Indiana. School days were extended to accommodate physical education programs and one-quarter of the hired teachers had appropriate training. Schoolyards began to change in landscape as outdoor exercise equipment was installed.[8,9] The practice began to spread to other North American cities. Play and playgrounds were formalized in organization and form.

During the decade following the founding of the PAA, the number of planned playgrounds spread rapidly. Now some six hundred communities across America could boast facilities with equipment such as swings, slides, seesaws, and sandboxes.

The period between the world wars, however, brought several changes. Recognition that play must address the developmental phases of different age groups led to the introduction of variety. Play areas for preschool children, some argued, must have different content than those for six- to fifteen-year-olds.

The Modern Movement had a profound effect on playground design. Modernists advocated a break with historical models. Problem-solving, the use of new materials, and fabrication methods were emphasized as appropriate activities for play.[4] A creator who implemented fledgling modernist ideas in the design of playgrounds and play equipment was Isamu Noguchi. Born in the United States and raised in Japan, Noguchi suggested replacement of flat playgrounds by small sandy hills equipped with slides and running water. He rethought equipment design and invented unconventional swings and spiral slides. Although he did not personally execute his concepts, the publication of Noguchi's ideas set the stage for new thinking in playground and equipment design, which took hold later in the century.

European playground development was similar in progress and design to that of North America until the 1940s. The devastation of World War II left many cities in ruins; the need to rebuild was urgent. A gifted designer and social reformer who contributed to the rebuilding of his own city and inspired designers elsewhere was the Dutch architect Aldo Van Eyck. Responsible for the design of seven hundred playgrounds in Amsterdam, Van Eyck sought to improve the daily life of children and to strengthen community ties. His goal was to foster connections among people by turning abandoned spaces into play areas and public hubs where both adults and kids could interact. He ignored past template design in favor of a site-specific approach. Special attention was paid to the needs of each neighborhood, inspiring residents from other parts of the city to demand similar interventions in theirs.[4]

In the Zaanhof playground, which measured 65 feet by 65 feet (20 meters by 20 meters) and was built in 1948, Van Eyck introduced four play situations: a circular sandbox, three climbing bars, seven jumping stones, and a roundabout. For each of the activities, a different floor shape and surface was created. Separate areas for adults with benches and trees were assigned on the yard's borders.[10] Another of Van Eyck's novelties was to eliminate the tall fences that enclosed playgrounds of earlier decades. Once the demarcation disappeared, the space became an integral part of the surrounding area. In addition, the park's surfacing materials were similar to those in the neighborhood around it to help it fit in with its context. Concrete cylinders of different heights were placed in the sandpit for children to use in play. There was a water fountain and tubular steel climbing arches, all designed by Van Eyck, and replicated around the world.

The Adventure Playground was a notable European development that challenged convention. The concept was introduced in 1943 by architect C. T. Sorensen in the Endrup section of Copenhagen. He sought to provide rural play opportunities for urban children through the use of natural materials. On the site, a play leader handed participants scraps of wood, metal, or masonry, as well as basic tools with which they were free to construct the fruits of their imagination in a collaborative effort. It was a significant deviation from the earlier, meticulously designed play spaces. The inclusion of trained guides made it a unique educational experience, and with media attention, the concept transferred to other European sites and to the U.S. By 1977, Adventure Playgrounds were to be found in some twenty American cities. Unfortunately, they did not catch the interest of municipal officials, because of the lack of funding to support the hiring of play leaders, which were essential to their success. Concern that such play presented a safety hazard, and authorities would be sued, did not help. The playgrounds were deemed unsightly by city managers and nearby residents, bringing an end to the idea.[11]

The post-World War II years in North America brought another phase in the evolution of playgrounds by establishing relationships between play equipment, its setting, and art. These ideas stemmed from the realization that equipment can be designed as *objets d'art*. They not only serve for play, but can also educate and inspire artistic endeavors among children. The company Play Sculptures was founded in 1951 by Frank Caplan and Bernard Barenholtz to engage sculptors in the creation of play artefacts. The firm enlisted Robert Winston to work on prototypes which were published a year later.

The free-flowing shapes were imaginative and colorful and broke the mold set by earlier designers. Other artists, including well known European creators, were invited to propose new shapes for the delight of children and adults.

Design of playgrounds benefited from the development of new materials and production techniques. Molded color plastic objects began to be showcased throughout the 1960s and 1970s. Plastic parts were combined with more traditional products, such as wood and steel, to form play structures. Colorful slides, both conventional and tubular, made their appearance as well.

In the decades that followed, there were innovations in playground landscapes and equipment design. Music gardens, where children explored sound-making gadgets, storybook places with play structures shaped after known literary characters, water parks that engaged kids in summer fun, and agriculture parks where they could take part in farming activities were introduced. The rising popularity of skateboards and the desire of city officials to move their use away from municipal property led to the building of skateboard parks.

The rudimentary playground with swing, sandbox, and a climbing structure has seen a decline in use and in some cases disappeared altogether. A rise in competing interests among children of most ages, shifting social attitudes, and new urban planning trends are the culprits.

In *The Disappearance of Childhood*, author Neil Postman noted that "Like distinctive forms of dress, children's games, once so visible on the streets of our towns, are also disappearing."[12] He refers to informal games that require no instructor, umpires, or spectators. Pointing to the sharp rise in the amount of time children spend watching television, he suggests that "every medium of communication that plugs into a wall socket has contributed its share in freeing children from the limited range of childhood sensibility." The rise of electronic media and the proliferation of information appliances in children's bedrooms have contributed to the decline of outdoor play. Studies indicate that TV viewing is North American youth's primary activity for 1.5 to 2.5 hours per day on average. Research indicates that TV rarely offers positive developmental experiences and that viewing is associated with developmental liabilities.[13]

An Austrian survey reported that around 80 percent of boys and 70 percent of girls use computers to play alone.[14] Play has not only changed location and moved indoors, but has profoundly altered in character to become stationary, passive to a large measure, and individual. Personal exchange after school hours, when it occurs, takes place online and face-to-face encounters happen on-screen through cameras.

Another influence with negative effects on children's play was, interestingly, their parents. Although time spent with children, primarily young ones at home, has increased compared to twenty years ago, time spent in activities that involve going somewhere together has declined.[15] The rise in time spent at work and engagement in media-related activities like Internet-surfing and TV-watching at home reduce the amount of time spent with children in outdoor activities. Studies point out that mothers share an average of 3.5 hours per day with their children, while fathers share 2.0 hours per day.[16]

The change in town planning traditions that began as the North American suburb came into being has transformed neighborhood landscapes and their playgrounds. Residential developers were required in most jurisdictions to set aside 10 percent of their land for public open space including parks and play spaces. There was little guidance as to how this area would be distributed and no insistence, for example, that small playgrounds be placed near clusters of homes. Developers favored large parks and playing fields to be used by many households since big swaths of land are more efficient to maintain than many smaller spots. The "culture of big" found its way into play areas as well. Playgrounds were often sited on the edge of neighborhoods, beyond most small children's walking or cycling reach. Parents might consider that going there alone was unsafe, and kids had to be driven to play. To coordinate activities for everyone, play and games had to be organized. Soccer, baseball, and football leagues sprouted up across North America, with young ones running in the field and parents watching and cheering from the sidelines. Play was boxed into time slots, losing its spontaneity.

Another change was brought about by our dwelling choices. Whereas prior to World War II, many North Americans resided in city apartments, single-family homes became the preferred home in suburbia. Many large backyards even had space for private swimming pools, further drawing children away from public spots. In winter, backyard skating rinks might be created. The growing consumer appetite led to another offering: the miniature playground. People could purchase inexpensive slides, seesaws, and swings for indoor or outdoor use. The very young had even less play time in public places.

The effect of indoor isolation and inactivity has been studied and documented in recent years. According to the American Academy of Pediatrics, by the age of eighteen, a child has seen an estimated three hundred and sixty thousand ads and two hundred thousand violent acts on television.[17] Many of the advertisements are placed by the food industry, which spends billions on advertising. Two-thirds of total advertising was by food processors, 28 percent by the food service industry (mostly fast-food restaurants), and 8 percent by food stores. Many of the ads encouraged children to eat fatty, salty, and sugary food.[18, 19]

Time spent watching television, playing computer games, and surfing the net, combined with poor dietary choices, has led to an increased risk of being overweight among children between seven and eleven years of age, compared to those who participate in physical activities or sports.[20] In 2000-2001, close to 5 percent of Canadian children twelve to nineteen years old were considered obese, with the prevalence of boys being twice that of girls.[21] Physicians agree that most of these children will encounter weight-related health problems as adults.

Internet addiction is affecting children's well-being. Studies show that even a few hours a week online led to a "deterioration of social and psychological life" and increased depression and sense of isolation in subjects who were otherwise normal.[19] Richard Louv, author of books on child development, including *Last Child in the Woods*, coined the phrase "nature-deficient disorder" to describe the possible effect on children, which hinders both their mental and physical development.[22]

Will we be able to draw kids away from television sets and computer screens? Can outdoor play be made relevant again?

Changing behavioral attitudes, habits, and norms takes time, but it is possible if consistent effort is made for a prolonged period. In the case of outdoor play, schools, media, and parents need to lead by example and promote healthy lifestyles. Changes are required in the way we plan communities. If in past decades we engineered play spaces and equipment to render them inaccessible to local neighborhoods, we ought to sketch them right back in. Much like the *shikun* in which I spent my childhood, small parks need to be built near clusters of homes with pathways permitting safe access on foot or by bicycle. When the distance to play spaces is long, streets need to be designed to calm traffic using planter boxes, speed bumps, and wide sidewalks. Some streets at certain seasons or times of day can be closed off to cars altogether. More should be done to bring about innovation for new playground concepts, including design competitions, for example, that may engage once again the artistic community. And there can be old-fashioned community get-togethers in local parks with organized activities. Parents, as well, must accompany their youngsters, participate, and demonstrate that the best interaction among people takes place face-to-face and not on Facebook.

As I surveyed the park where Shalom Lev and I stood, I noticed that it felt a bit awkward to return to a place of childhood memories in the company of a friend from that time. But as we reminisced, pointing out features of the scene and recalling names, it became clear that we had been fortunate. We had a good time in this neighborhood, and it molded who we became as adults.

Seven

Wandering in Tijuana

~

"IT IS A MAQUILADORA," MANUEL ROSEN told me when I asked him about a large boxy white structure on a distant hilltop as we drove through the outskirts of Tijuana, Mexico. "Large multinational corporations build assembly plants which draw to the area job seekers, mostly poor migrants from southern states," he added.

I had come to Tijuana, which touches Mexico's border with the U.S. just below San Diego, at the invitation of Rosen, Director of the School of Architecture at the Universidad Iberoamericana Noroeste. He had heard about my affordable housing work and suggested that I share my knowledge with his students. After my talk, he offered to show me one of the many squatter settlements that bordered the city.

As the car turned a corner, I saw hundreds, maybe thousands of brown spots covering the surrounding hills. It was difficult at first to make out what they were. As we got closer, though, I could see that they were shacks. I hoped they were abandoned, remnants of a past disaster, until I noticed that there were people going in and out of these homes and ramshackle cars driving among them. Rosen noted the expression on my face and explained that new arrivals stay with relatives or rent at first, then they squat on a lot. By themselves or with the help of friends, they construct a place on evenings or weekends. Later, informal electrical connections are made and years later, just before elections, a water pipe would be laid, he added with a smile.

We turned onto a dirt road and parked. A few months earlier, the region had been inundated by severe flooding. A washed-out bridge was replaced by two large logs with scraps of wood between them. A woman carrying bags crossed, timidly. Rosen pointed to an eatery in a wooden structure with palm branches covering a porch, under which a variety of tables and chairs were arranged, and suggested we sit. A man wearing an apron stood behind the counter. At the rear, in shadow, I could see a girl dipping dishes into a large barrel full of soapy water. We ordered and took our food to one of the tables, dining quietly. The owner approached and asked if all was to our liking, and engaged Rosen in a conversation. I said I'd like to walk around a bit, and left.

I strolled through a narrow unpaved path between a row of shacks with improvised electric wire overhead. Sewage, streaming in a side ditch, smelled bad. Many worn tires were being used to hold back eroding soil or to serve as front stairs. A large tanker truck arrived at an intersection and stopped. Women stepped out of their homes, filled up an assortment of plastic containers and buckets, paid the driver, and carried the water into their homes.

The dwellings had walls made out of planks of wood covered with tar paper, and rusty corrugated sheet metal roofs. The main doors and most windows looked as if they had seen better days and clearly had been recycled. Red bricks were piled near one house, waiting for reuse. Someone was building a cinderblock addition to a wooden structure next door. The area looked like a sluggish yet active giant building site.

A woman came out of one of the houses, which was adorned with a large sign, and greeted me. I climbed from the dirt road to her home, which was clad with corrugated metal sheets painted green. Geraniums and mint grew in old pickle cans beside the wall. The front of the structure served as a grocery store. Canned foods were neatly arranged on one wooden shelf, packages of toilet paper on another. Everything looked spotless. The door to the back room was open, and I could see through to the living space inside. I made out a number of functions in a room no larger than 15 feet by 15 feet (4.6 meters by 4.6 meters). There was a small kitchen counter with a sink supplied with water from an overhead plastic pipe extended from a container. A bucket was placed below to collect grey water. A single bed with a baby's crib beside it took up one corner. Another corner had a table and four chairs. One section of the room was partitioned off with a cloth, behind which I could see a double bed, probably the parents' zone. I pointed to a package of gum, paid, nodded to the smiling woman, and stepped out.

It was my first encounter with poverty on such an enormous scale. The squatters were here because they had no choice. The desire to better their lives had driven them from poorer southern regions "al Norte", to the North. As I looked back at the shop from which I had just exited and the endless rows of shacks around me, with the piles of brick and worn-out windows, doors, and tires, it occurred to me that I was in the midst of a huge recycling operation. It was a rudimentary manifestation of people building their shelter out of anything they could lay their hands on.

Despite the poverty, I felt that the place had a soul, an uncommon sense of place, perhaps drawn from the manifest absence of means.

I felt ashamed of the excessive consumption that we northerners engage in. I almost felt like apologizing. It made me wonder whether our striving to own more, with that bloated, sluggish, and unfulfilled feeling that results from the effort to keep up with the Joneses, creates better places. Has our consumption rate spun out of control? Do we truly understand the consequences of our habits—their effect on the environment, for example?

There is no better place to reflect on contemporary habits than in our residences.

Since the middle of the twentieth century, homes have become the target of marketing by many industries, such as the electronic, information, and even food manufacturing. We are not helpless victims of those enterprises, but rather willing participants. The drive to have more, different, or better makes people work harder in the hope that additional "stuff" will make them happy. But we soon discover that the thrill disappears once the acquisition is made, and so the cycle begins again.

The ability of the middle class to own a single-family home was hailed as one of the greatest post-World War II North American achievements. Tract houses with few amenities were meant to satisfy the basic needs of a young household. This modest beginning, it was argued, would become a stepping stone towards acquisition of larger, better-equipped dwellings. And indeed it has. In 1943, an average North American home measured 75 square meters (800 square feet.). The average new home had grown to 100 square meters (1,100 square feet) by 1955. The mid-1980s marked the arrival of the baby boomers to the home-buying market. The average new single-family home in most markets was close to 200 square meters (about 2,000 square feet). This expansion paralleled a decrease in the size of an average household, from 3.7 members in 1971 to 2.7 in 2006. We simply reduced our crowding. Our disposable incomes, on the other hand, increased. Double-income families had more money to spend on homes, but less time to spend in them, as the number of hours spent at the office rose. To compensate for a stressful lifestyle and to demonstrate the fruit of hard work, home buyers sought greater domestic comfort.

The construction and building products industries have, obviously, promoted these trends along with other marketers. The home became a vehicle for the acquisition of goods and services appearing in more and more seductive wrapping. In 2003, almost 25 percent of Canadian households owned three or more television sets, and almost 33 percent used two or more refrigerators, for example. Furthermore, 67 percent of the primary refrigerators and 35 percent of the secondary refrigerators owned were considered large, with capacities greater than 16.4 cubic feet (0.46 cubic meters).[1] The media bring to our attention the existence of these "improved" appliances, enticing us directly or indirectly to buy them. We are influenced by fictional people's homes in movies and on television shows, and by interior decor magazines. Buying is simpler, with easy access to credit. We can browse home shopping channels and online networks. Consumption has become superficial, impulsive, as we have eliminated the thought from the act.

Contemporary residential design reflects this. Within a given income level and demographic, new developments strive to seem distinctive from one another. Yet, paradoxically, they all have the same basic interior with the same attention-grabbing features. Appreciation of craftsmanship has been replaced by the objective of impressing with size. A new home may feature a huge foyer, high ceilings, larger windows, curving staircases, and fireplaces destined never to be used. In fact, a new home today is a parade of wonders. Take the kitchen, for example. The microwave oven led the transformation of the kitchen from a cooking to a processing place. It changed our food buying from raw ingredients to ready-to-serve products, changing the need for storage space. Bigger fridges replaced pantries stocked with staples and preserves. The size and number of kitchen cabinets and counter space increased to accommodate food processors, juicers, pasta machines, automatic bread makers, popcorn poppers, cappuccino machines, and other appliances that we get as Christmas, wedding, or housewarming gifts, or which we buy to satisfy a romantic idea after watching a cooking show, some of which we only use once and then bury deep inside a lower cabinet.

Clever marketing has transformed the bathroom. This once-humble space now boasts a veritable spa of appliances: whirlpool bath, multi-jet shower, quiet-flush toilet, double-sink counter with rows of theatre make-up lights, all vie for our attention in an Italian-tiled paradise. There is the main bathroom, the first-floor powder room, another on the basement level, and the ensuite in the master bedroom. Statistics show that the average American household consumes approximately 409 U.S. gallons (1,550 liters) of water per day. Outdoor irrigation accounts for 20 to 50 percent of residential water use depending on climate zone. According to the American Water Works Association, the average house contains two or three toilets. Each of them has an average of twelve to thirteen flushes per day.[2]

Although the depletion of freshwater resources is not considered to be an imminent threat in many areas of North America, over-consumption in the residential sector contributes to major waste water management problems in most municipalities that treat wastewater from homes before it is released back into the ecosystem. Municipal treatment centers consume large amounts of energy and are limited in the amount of waste water that can be treated at a given time. Since many municipalities treat storm water and sewage together, when the system is overloaded by water from a storm, even where there is sewage treatment, overflow may be accidentally released untreated.

Of course, in this digital age the electronics and entertainment industries have affected domestic consumption. Providers of telephone and cable companies recognized the potential in transforming the home into a long-term service consumer. Computers have become a necessity, as services such as online banking and shopping appear on the Internet. In most homes, one computer doesn't seem to be enough; children do homework, play games, and surf the net, and parents catch up on office work and go online to read the news, pay bills, or check on the performance of their stocks.

Cable TV, pay-per-view, and satellite access to hundreds of channels have turned living rooms into "home theatres" with huge screens and surround sound. Segmentation of television broadcasting has led to the purchase of DVD players and a second, or even a third TV set. Our vinyl LPs have gone the way of the eight-track tape (remember those?), rendered obsolete by CDs and their required players and now by personal digital players with headsets. Consumers have little say as High-Definition TV and newer video technologies become the standard.

Wall Street wants us to believe that consumer spending is a welcome, positive indicator of how we are faring as individuals. Governments regard consumer confidence as a vital sign of national economic well-being. In reality, none of these agencies shares with us the real cost of senseless consumption. What we are not fully aware of, or often chose to ignore, is the effect of the many faces of excessive consumption on the environment, and indirectly on people like those whom I saw in Tijuana.

AVI FRIEDMAN

The causes of environmental phenomena such as global warming, depletion of natural resources, excessive consumption, and
waste generation relate to several sectors. Close examination of the
data shows that the residential sector follows the industrial and
transportation sectors in energy consumption, for example.[3] Along
with expansion in home size, energy consumption has grown.
According to the U.S. Energy Information Administration, energy
consumption in the residential sector rose from 14,930 trillion BTUs
to 21,879 trillion BTUs between 1973 and 2005.[4] Since some 60 percent of the total energy consumed in the residential sector is used
for space heating, the energy rise can be attributed to an increase in
home size, the number of windows installed, and poor construction
practices.

It can also be attributed to a number of features that have
become standard in the modern home. Air conditioners are large
energy consumers and emitters of chlorofluorocarbon refrigerants.
Statistics show that 45 percent of Canadian households made use
of some sort of air conditioning unit in 2003, compared with 25 percent in 1993.[5] Some attribute the increase to hotter than average
summers, while others argue that this is just another manifestation
of the rise in North American household consumption. Central air
conditioners consume in one cooling season roughly the same
amount of energy as the annual consumption of a refrigerator,
range, and clothes dryer combined.

The ever-expanding size of our homes takes a bite of another
natural resource: solid sawn lumber. Considered to be an inexpensive, renewable resource with relatively low energy requirements,
wood has become the material of choice over light-gauge steel in
house building. According to a 2006 report by the Nebraska Energy
Office, the amount of lumber necessary to build a 1,700-square-
foot (160-square-meter) wood-frame home, including its structure
and finishes, consumes 1 acre (0.4 hectares) of forest.[6] The figure
becomes even more staggering when you consider that some two
million dwelling units are constructed each year in the United States
alone and approximately two hundred thousand in Canada.

The building process is responsible for a large amount of waste generation. Some 8,000 pounds (3.6 metric tons) of waste is produced when a 2,000-square foot (190-square-meter) home is constructed, all of which is shipped to landfills.

How should we then design, build, and use our homes? We simply need to learn to live within our means, that is, within the limits of the natural resources available to sustain our existence on earth. The proliferation of the term "sustainable development" and the conditions that brought it about can be traced back to the mid-1970s. In 1972 the United Nations Conference on the Human Environment in Stockholm focused on how we are stretching the carrying capacity of the earth to its limits.[7] The meeting served as a podium for the first international discussion on the relationship between ongoing environmental depletion and damage and the future of humanity. It was recognized then that population growth in some nations and over-consumption in others could not be sustained indefinitely, and that development practices leave noticeable footprints in the form of land degradation, deforestation, air pollution, and water scarcity. The Stockholm meeting led to the establishment of a number of international organizations whose actions put in place mechanisms that disseminated findings about the deteriorating state of the environment and recommended appropriate actions.

These initiatives laid the foundation for several widely accepted views, the main one being that the stock of non-renewable resources on Earth is finite.[8] Years later, this reflection has led to the establishment of the World Commission on Environment and Development, also referred to as the Brundtland Commission, which is probably the best-known international initiative. In the report *Our Common Future* the commissioners defined sustainable development as "development that meets present needs without compromising the ability of future generations to meet their own needs." This definition established a conceptual approach to development, whereby any action taken must be pursued with its future effects in mind.[9]

AVI FRIEDMAN

What should our guiding principles for design be? Learning from the squatters of Tijuana, who unfortunately are not doing it by choice, to minimize consumption of natural resources should be first on our minds. When any resources have to be used, rather than consume non-renewable ones, we should use renewable resources that can be replenished through a relatively rapid natural cycle. When non-renewables have to be considered, we should use those that can be recycled, including all non-energy mineral resources that are extracted from the earth's crust, such as ores of copper, aluminum, nickel, and other metals and minerals. As these minerals are mined, they are not replaced, yet they can be collected and recycled. A good place to begin a talk about recycling and the contribution that each of us can make is in the home where, ideally, 32 percent of all waste can be recycled and turned into building products.

A visit to a conscientious builder's residential construction site shows how successful recycling programs can be. It demonstrates that builders can help keep the planet clean, even though switching to environmentally-friendly building products has not been an easy process. Products must meet building standards regarding fire-rating, strength, and durability, and be financially competitive with traditional products to be adopted by tradesmen and buyers alike. Some new products have gradually found their way into different parts of the home and their numbers are steadily growing.

Exterior wall insulation is an area in which recycled products have been making significant inroads. One of the chief products used is paper, which accounts for 21 percent of domestic waste. The most common type of recycled paper is newsprint. Recycling newsprint not only decreases air pollution emissions by up to 74 percent, but also uses 58 percent less water than converting virgin wood pulp to paper. It uses up to 50 percent less energy and saves millions of trees each year. The newsprint is chopped into small pieces, mixed with a bonding agent, and blown into the wall cavity to become an insulation buffer. Known as cellulose insulation, it can replace fiberglass insulation in the roof, where it's easier to

88

handle and install. Recycled paper can be found in roofing paper, shingles, and gypsum wallboard.

Some 50 to 100 percent of new steel products contain recycled scrap metal. Scrap was traditionally recovered from industrial waste, automobiles, and the demolition of steel structures, but in recent years, it has begun to include products from municipal solid waste. Empty cans put in recycling boxes are turned into light-gauge metal studs that are becoming common for use in interior partitions. They are light and will not warp, and electricians like them because, unlike wood studs, using metal studs means they do not need to drill holes to pass wires through. The wallboard that covers the studs is, in turn, made of recycled gypsum mixed with fibers that strengthen the board. And the boards do not need a paper facing, which makes for a smoother finishing process and appearance.

Recycled plastics, which account for 5 percent of domestic waste and 21 percent of total landfill volume, are being sought after as a construction material. Reusing plastic containers for the food industry is too expensive, but they can be used for manufacturing building products. For example, interior or exterior carpets made from plastic are indistinguishable from conventional carpets, come in a range of shades and patterns, and are cost-competitive. Recycled plastic is being converted into decking boards, outdoor handrails, stairs, street benches, and planter boxes.[10]

The more than three hundred million car tires that are discarded each year in North America have become the target of intense recycling. Old tires are breeding grounds for disease carriers such as mosquitoes and rodents, and they constitute a serious safety hazard, especially if they catch fire ,because extinguishing tire fires is extremely difficult. Recycled tires have already found their way into driveways, sidewalks, and paths in the form of interlocking pavers, and into living rooms as carpet underpads.

Can excessive use of resources and avoidance of recycling affect a sense of place? It certainly can, but not necessarily in our immediate environment. The resources that we use are often harvested in remote locations, with serious impacts on the physical environment.

When trees are clear-cut in faraway forests, natural habitat is ruined and waterways are polluted. Permanent scars are left in the earth's crust where surface mining takes place.

I had no doubt that the squatters of Tijuana wished for a better life and nicer homes. But they taught me a valuable lesson: we can all live with less.

Eight

E-mails from Broughton Hall

ROGER TEMPEST GREETED ME in his Broughton Hall office. The casually-dressed Yorkshireman pointed to an aerial photo of his 3,000 acre (1,200 hectare) estate, located between Yorkshire and Lancashire near the town of Skipton, England. In the photo, I could see a large building and several clusters of small ones.

Minutes later, we were on a tour of the place. His dark green Land Rover rattled over a cobblestone road and stopped in front of the mansion that I had seen in the photo. The origins of his family, he told me, could be traced to 1098. In 1597, one of his forefathers, Stephen Tempest, commissioned the main building in Elizabethan style to house his large family. Generations of Tempests have lived here ever since, with the exception of a brief period in 1644 when the Hall was requisitioned by Oliver Cromwell.

The car rolled on through pathways carved into the beautifully tended lush green lawns dotted with budding spring shrubs and tall trees. After a short drive, we passed under an arched building and stopped in a paved courtyard. "It all began in the stable block," he noted. "In 1981, after a period of slow and steady economic decline and inability to maintain those structures, my father, who took over the estate following the death of his brother, let this building out to a Norwegian company designing North Sea oil rigs. "The rest," he smiled, "is history." We recognized that office work no longer needs to be done in a downtown glass tower and that contemporary communications technology lets one work from anywhere, even from a small structure in a British estate. In 1985, I took over and converted more buildings to offices and built new ones."

After a short drive, we arrived at the Home Park, where I saw the Pinetum, Gillow, and Griffin houses, which in earlier times had housed staff who tended to the estate and their families.

"We also offer supplementary services and facilities to companies who rent space in Broughton Hall," Tempest added. "These include on-site food catering, a fitness center, meeting and training rooms, and a garden pavilion designed by Sir Michael Hopkins to host conferences."

We left the main estate area and drove to the Water Mill Park, where stone-clad buildings form a paved square around a flower-shaped stone water fountain in the center. "The main structure served as a corn mill," Tempest explained. "The court is a true manifestation of the Industrial Revolution, with water wheels, steam engines, and coal gas production. Perhaps it is a metaphor for a new phase in the revolution of business and industry, the cyber one." Tempest invited me to visit a building where I saw a modern interior in stark contrast to the old articulated stone exterior. In a large open space divided by low partitions, people faced computers under a ceiling made up of heavy wooden beams. "We currently have on the estate companies involved in electronic design, cruise ship management, and animated imaging, which offer services to faraway clients," he remarked.

We stepped out into the courtyard and a late morning sun. I tried to imagine how this place had looked centuries ago with people stepping out of the water mill carrying bags of flour. Broughton Hall, I realized, is not only a successful business idea, but a manifestation of the changing nature of office work. The firms that have chosen to locate in the estate have done so because of the magnificent setting, which stands in marked contrast to where clerical work has been located in the past half century, the heart of cities. I wondered, however, how this transformation has affected the workers. Has the new work environment altered relationships among colleagues? Have we made information technology the center our working lives? What is next for office design?

The hierarchy of essential human needs, work among them,

was identified by psychologist Abraham Maslow in 1943. People first seek to satisfy their basic physiological needs, then safety require-ments, then the need for social acceptance and esteem, and at the highest level, the quest for self-fulfillment. Maslow's hierarchy is regarded as universally encompassing human behavior in Western culture, including people's attitudes to work.

Some assume, incorrectly, that offices and clerical work are modern inventions. Earlier civilizations laid the foundation of many of the principles employed in today's work environment. To control their vast territory and many undertakings, ancient Egyptians established an impressive bureaucracy. Functionaries oversaw food supply, as well as huge engineering, infrastructure, and monument-building projects. Organized along hierarchical structures, clerks and bookkeepers were in charge of transcribing all records. It was suggested that some moved around to verify facts and give orders while others labored in permanent spots.[1] In cities like Amarna, archaeologists excavated a structure that took up several city blocks and was used for Egyptian royal correspondence.[2]

The ancient Greeks organized their bureaucracy in smaller units. The headquarters was located in a multifunctional hall at the agora, each town's socio-political center. In addition to shared space for all workers, there were cellular rooms for high-ranking officials, as well as meeting spaces. The Roman cities established bureaucracies called *opera liberi* (the work of freemen). Holding such an office was regarded as a mark of absolute freedom. The main center was located in the forum and, like the Greeks, the Romans went on to develop typical floor plans for their offices. There were designs for town halls and villas for each administrative district. Private enterprises flourished in the city of Rome, including a financial sector in the Basilicas Aemilla and Julia. They offered services resembling today's banks.

After the fall of the Roman Empire, it took until the twelfth century for commerce and trade to flourish within Europe. Trade led to the establishment of advanced administrations for both public and private sectors. In the late Middle Ages the foundation of our present financial institutions was set in place. Derived from the Latin word *banchi*, a money-changer's table, banks offered a variety of services to local enterprises which needed changes of currencies or loans. Banking was formalized in organization and space design in the fifteenth century.

The Medici dynasty became Europe's largest merchant banker. They housed staff in central, formal city offices. Noted for expanding his family's fortunes and establishing Florence as a hub of trade, Cosimo de' Medici carried out sweeping reforms and constructed the Uffizi Galleries. The U-shaped, three-story building was designed by Giorgio Vasari in 1560 and resembled a Greek stoa, with a series of individual buildings accessed via a first-floor colonnade. When opened, it housed thirteen institutions, including public authorities and guild offices, and had a main reception hall. The Uffizi can be considered the prototype of the contemporary office building.[3]

A century later, in 1694, expanding trade led to the establishment of the first European state central bank in England, which moved on to its own headquarters in London a few years afterward. Designed to accommodate different functions, it was organized into a hierarchy of cashiers, bookkeepers, and supervising directors. Employees sat in a vast hall next to a long row of tables arranged in parallel, which became the model for office space until the twentieth century.[4]

The Industrial Revolution influenced the formalization of clerical work. Manufacturing conglomerates required large areas to manage their affairs. The need for office space in cities like London and Manchester mushroomed rapidly. Institutions such as banks, insurance companies, and civil administrations needed to accommodate their growing operations.

A fundamental change which began during the Renaissance was the separation between home and work. For safety reasons, new zoning regulations prohibited the mix of certain land uses which, once more, placed additional demand on scarce spaces.

In the U.S. after the end of the Civil War, businesses began to expand. Derived from a military term, many newly established "companies" began to operate. Employees were hired to perform a variety of clerical tasks, such as coordination of long-distance distribution networks and marketing strategies. The 1860 census showed that 750,000 people were engaged in such services. The number rose to 2,160,000 in 1890 and to 4,420,000 in 1910.[5]

Private corporations and banks began to play an important role in many countries' economies. Their growing fortunes were invested in building headquarters and satellite offices designed to accommodate bureaucratic efficiencies. Many new office buildings in the U.S. and Europe had similar exteriors and interiors arranged in one of three main patterns: office rooms on either side of central corridors, grouped around an atrium, or surrounding a single central room. Having a private cellular office rather than sharing open space with others became a status symbol within a firm. Management methods emerged, leading to an agglomeration of departments by function and inter-collaboration.

Advancements in construction technology gave a boost to office building design. Development of reinforced concrete and steel-beam structures was instrumental in permitting creation of large open areas, free of columns, with greater interior flexibility. The invention of the elevator by Elisha Otis in 1853 eliminated the height limit. Companies could now concentrate their entire operation in one tall building and arrange departments by floor, leading to greater efficiency, rather than locate them in one or several spread-out edifices. Chicago, a city associated with the proliferation of the skyscraper, led the way in office design. Tall buildings with column-free floor spaces laid the foundation for contemporary open-plan work spaces.

Nineteenth-century smaller-scale office innovation and furnishing design were instrumental in changing the office environment. Electricity not only powered elevators, but illuminated spaces. Reliance on daytime natural light was no longer absolute as employees could now have artificial lighting above or on their desks. The invention of the telephone altered office operations markedly. By carrying voice over wires, the telephone undercut the hierarchies of "military-style organizations" and heightened individual power.[6] Patented by Alexander Graham Bell in 1876, the telephone was expanded by Theodore Vail of AT&T, who grasped its potential for office work and developed it into a network system. Although people were slow to adopt it at first, the number of telephone users grew to ten million in the three decades following its introduction. What led to its being embraced by enterprises was the ability given to head offices to establish communications with, and control of, satellite offices. It enabled responses to public inquiries, which increased business activities and changed operational methods.

Two inventions which affected clerical work were the newly designed desk and the typewriter. Know first as a "writing table", the first office desks were highly cumbersome, yet their designers paid attention both to the tasks performed by and the storage needs of an employee. The notion of targeted accessories designed for a specific job was born when Frank Lloyd Wright designed the furnishings, desks included, for his 1906 Larkin Building in Buffalo, New York. He provided drawings for a ground-level public service desk and for desks for clerical workers and executives. Desks manufactured of metal were an innovation of the Van Dorn Iron Works of Cleveland, which later went on to develop metal filing cabinets.[6]

Desk development paralleled the typewriter. The concept was based on the idea of interchangeable parts that was pioneered for firearms by the Remington Company in 1874. Typewritten documents were not welcomed at first, as they got confused with printed press material and were considered too impersonal. The acceptance of typewriters imposed other standards on office work in America, including the adoption of 8.5 by 11 inches (216 by 280 millimeters) as the standard size for a letter and for filing folders and their storage cabinets.

These technologies served as a backdrop to new methods aimed at increasing office efficiency. A pivotal book on the subject was Fredrick W. Taylor's *The Principles of Scientific Management*, published in 1911.[6] Taylor argued for design to support increased productivity. Office planning was no longer regarded as an exercise in fitting spaces with rooms or desks, but as creating task- and output-related arrangements based on the employees' capabilities and efficiency. New operational thinking became paramount in office design.

Wright's Larkin Building, designed to house 1,800 employees, is considered North America's first office environment to integrate architectural innovation with a progressive management philosophy, advanced utility systems, spatial arrangements, and furniture design. It had a unique communication and distribution system, and offered social amenities and activities to its employees, most of whom were women. The clerical work force sat in an open gallery in a large six-story atrium in long rows of small desks opposite each other.

Research into office efficiency over the first three decades of the twentieth century further contributed to the transformation of office design and work. Specialization of tasks, systematization of work, and maximization of efficiency became the leading concepts. These principles were expressed in Frank Lloyd Wright's design for the Johnson Wax building in 1936. The company's fifteen departments were placed in a huge, naturally-lit hall.

With the increased participation of clerical workers in the labor force, office workers began to distinguish themselves from factory workers, who wore blue-collar shirts, by wearing white ones that went on to become an international status symbol.

During the Great Depression of the 1930s and World War II, construction of new office buildings came to a halt. Innovation returned after the war with a vengeance, and in the 1950s function, form, and efficiency were at their highest. The modern office tower quickly became a symbol of the corporation, with its local and even global economic influence. A change occurred in the contribution that architects made to office environments. Whereas earlier architects had aimed to improve the organization of office work, newer generations concentrated on designing advanced building envelopes, leaving interior arrangements to other disciplines. Improving efficiency by optimizing operational relations between departments remained central in the thinking of interior designers.

The International Style paid little homage to a building's local urban context or its internal environment. It compensated for this lack of attention with the increased use of artificial light and central air conditioning. Similar-looking edifices with glass or aluminum curtain wall exteriors and partition-free interior spaces were constructed worldwide. One such building was the 1954 Seagram Building in New York. The architect was modernist Ludwig Mies van der Rohe. It has a large front plaza at street level and a spacious lobby, and is notable for its wide expanses of glass and steel columns. It became the prototypical contemporary office tower.

An investigation in 1959 into patterns of office organization by the West German Quickborner team brought about a rethinking of interior office design once more. Studying the flow of paper-based and visual communication between individuals and groups resulted in *Bürolandschaft*, office landscaping. Implemented in a 1960 building for the Bertelsman Publishing Company at Gütersloh, it created a unique environment by incorporating opportunities for informal communication through quiet zones, meeting areas, and refreshment stations, all in close proximity to work stations. The system offered the possibility for easy alteration of layouts to accommodate shifts in tasks. Staff sat in a free-form pattern a short distance from their supervisor, and moved about easily. In addition to organizational ramifications, this arrangement fostered an atmosphere of hierarchy-free equality that fit into the mindset of the 1960s.[7]

The 1970s brought new concerns to the forefront. The 1973 oil crisis was a wake-up call which discouraged developers from relying on energy-consuming artificial lights and air conditioning. Noise associated with the open-plan concept seemed to outweigh its other advantages, and managers quickly retired to closed offices. A concept emerged which attempted to marry the advantage of open layout with that of a cellular office. Known as Combi-Office, it was implemented in the 1978 Canon office building in Solna, Sweden.

An invention that facilitated this approach was the Action Office system. It was developed in 1968 by Robert Probst, author of *The Office: A Facility Based on Change.* Working for the Herman Miller Corporation, Probst's idea was "that office furniture should be a kit of parts responding to the varied tasks of office work and recognizing the conflict between privacy and communication inherent in office organizations."[8] Space could now be arranged according to unique rapidly altered functions, and employees could select components that suited their specific chores from a kit.

The 1980s would launch office design into a new era known as the "PC Revolution". The introduction of the desktop personal computer in the late 1970s fundamentally changed the office landscape. Information technology demanded rethinking of office operations. The need to wire desktop and mainframe computers, printers, and fax machines required rethinking of floor and ceiling designs. The number of paper transactions declined as more data was transmitted and stored digitally. Corporations went on to engage IT specialists and allocate spaces for data processing equipment.

With parallel evolution in telephone technology, the rise of tele-conferencing enabled corporate personnel to meet from several spots simultaneously and redefined the term "meeting room".

The dawn of the information age permitted increased globalization of manufacturing and trade. Corporations still needed head offices, yet cyber communication closed the physical gap between faraway destinations. E-mails rendered the need for large mail rooms, a staple of nineteenth-century design, less important. High-speed fiber-optic cables and satellite telephony have led to the birth of call centers for customer service in low-wage countries. Digital networking permitted the outsourcing of tasks such as booking and marketing to other companies. It all led to the de-territorialization of work. It is now distributed around the world and performed around the clock.[9]

The communications revolution brought about a reduction in the importance of downtown as the location for office buildings. Companies began to move their head offices to suburbia, where they could find cheaper land or rent. They could easily access a qualified pool of labor, which migrated from the heart of cities. Roger Tempest started the Broughton Hall Business Park when he recognized that corporations no longer needed to be located downtown in nearby Leeds.

But now people don't even have to leave home. In the year 2000, the Henley Centre suggested that 4 percent of the U.K. workforce, 1.2 million people, were using their homes as offices at least part-time, and the father of telecommuting, Jack Nilles of California, reported that four million were doing so in the U.S.[10] The proliferation of home offices has not reduced the need for conventional office space.

Business models have continued to evolve. Reducing labor to the minimum has become part of corporate culture and is now considered a sound management practice. Impressed by Japanese systems, Western corporations began to emphasize task-based, process- and result-oriented teamwork. Teams are formed for the duration of specific projects. The profile of a "good" employee has changed from one who is diligent and obedient to one with social competence, communication skills, and the flexibility to shift between tasks along the project's life cycle. The team's head is no longer the authority, but a colleague, a cheerleader of sorts. Work can be carried out at all times of the day, according to bursts of innovation and the demands imposed by deadlines.

Invention of new information appliances coupled with contemporary approaches to management systems have given rise to new functions and meant further evolution in office layouts. The wireless age was ushered in around the dawn of the twenty-first century. The slogan is now "Your office is where you are!" Data can be sent from and received anywhere. Laptop computers and PDAs— personal digital assistants, also known as palmtop computers—can be carried anywhere and operated in all places with WiFi signals. Most have cameras that permit face-to-face two-way communication and exchange of data, reducing the need for meetings. Cellular phones and PDAs let one answer calls or surf the Internet at any time. The need for formal office space has become less relevant.

Our era is characterized by a new kind of relationship between companies and their employees. Whereas in the past workers were often employed by the same company throughout their entire working lives, now workers need to adapt to learning new skills and occasionally changing career paths or workplaces. Social benefits such as old age pensions, once the employer's responsibility, have now been left to the employee. Gender equality has broken down traditional stereotypes, leading to role changes in families.

What models are likely to emerge and what will the office of the future look like? Futurists often use the key word "flexibility". It is highly likely that interior layouts of offices will be rearranged several times during the edifice's life cycle. Flexibility will be needed to further accommodate information technologies yet to be invented. Broadly speaking, future appliances will be wireless, integrated, and essential. Office space is "greening" as environmental concerns are given higher priority. Reducing energy consumption, use of recycled construction materials, and limiting travel will be some of the measures taken.

And what about the employees? It is difficult to foresee how new designs and social trends will affect the well-being of office workers. People, many suggest, will be more mobile and versatile. Retiring baby boomers are likely to start new careers, perhaps based in home offices equipped with a multitude of digital gadgets. Based on trends already underway, new ideas in office design are described by Marilyn Zelinsky in her book *The Inspired Workspace*. In the Nurturing Workspace, people feel free to unwind, rest, and gather the energy needed to regroup in creative collaboration. Designed to simulate residential environments, such places will have amenities available at home. Workspaces of this kind have been created by the Swedish furnishing giant IKEA for several of its offices. In the company's Conshohocken, Pennsylvania U.S. headquarters, dining spaces look like cozy kitchens. There is an area with comfortable red sofas resembling a living room, and a library. Wireless Internet permits staff members to meet and work anywhere in the building and with entirely flexible work hours, they can do so, all day and night.[11]

Fantasy Workspaces are meant to transform employees by creating radically unique interiors that inspire creativity. Such is the case at Duffy Design, a New York City graphic company where employees who exit the elevator walk into a spaceship-like environment. At Google's headquarters in Mountain View, California, employees are given downtime spaces where they can pursue reading and sports in a fantasy-like decor. In Serene Workplaces, people find sanctuary and peace of mind. The intention is to create an atmosphere free of noise or other office-like distractions. Such spaces have been created for artists in Denmark and Germany.

It was late morning when Roger Tempest and I drove through a meticulously tended landscape to his main office. We passed old buildings on grassy knolls and trees which extended their branches over the road. I wondered how one would categorize such a work environment. Possibly as the future of the past.

Nine

The Winds of Fargo

~

It was a sunny, crisp, and frigid morning in February in Fargo, North Dakota. I stepped out of my hotel to walk to the city's historic core. Icy snow cracked under my feet. I had come to attend a conference which was to begin later. I arrived at First Avenue and paused at an intersection, wondering which direction I should take. Cars were waiting for the light to change, plumes of white vapor rising from their exhausts. The sidewalks were mostly deserted. Overhead, I spotted pedestrians in an enclosed skywalk leading to the Convention Center. A gust of cold north wind mixed with snow-flakes hit my face. I pulled my toque over my ears and zipped up my parka. Snow drifted across the wide asphalt road and mostly empty parking lots, turning them white. The facades of the buildings that lined the streets offered little comfort, but a cluster of old low-rise buildings to the west drew my attention and determined my path.

As I crossed Roberts Street and arrived at Tenth Avenue North, I felt the tips of my fingers in my gloves turning numb. I glanced at three- and four-story brick and stone buildings, designed in Classical Revival style. Walking in the bitter cold I wondered why European immigrants had settled here in the first place. When they did, was the Nordic location a consideration? How did early and contemporary planners take measures to adapt to Fargo's winter conditions?

From what I could see and feel on my brief stroll through the historic district, there was very little evidence that climate was on the mind of the city's forefathers. It has a grid layout, the heritage of centuries-old Greek towns and Roman settlements. That was the pattern upon which many European cities were built and it was probably brought here by the first European settlers. The rectangular grid funnels the wind down oversized empty streets, often piling snow against walls. There was no sign that summer conditions were on their minds either. Fargo was founded in 1875 as a stopping point for steamboats travelling down the Red River. The town began flourishing when the railroad linked it with the East. Originally named "Centralia", it was renamed Fargo after Northern Pacific Railway director and Wells Fargo Express Company founder William Fargo.

The first people who roamed the western plains were First Nations Indians. Archaeological digs trace the presence of hunting colonies to a period after the retreat of the glaciers about ten thousand years ago. Later settlements of hunter-gatherers as well as farming people date to 2,000 B.C. When the first white explorers arrived at what is now North Dakota, they met members of the Dakota or Lakota nations, among other tribes, who moved into the northern Red River Valley and hunted in the western Buffalo range.

Standing in the heart of historic downtown Fargo, unable to spot a building or a dense formation of coniferous trees to break the wind, I wondered why the first white settlers had not begun planning by learning from the experience gained over centuries by aboriginal tribes. Ancient societies can offer a valuable lesson about relating habitat to a chosen form and place of settlement. It was common to select local materials and use them appropriately, while considering weather conditions. Unlike Western cultures, Native societies respected and worked *with* nature rather than against it. They did not attempt to impose their habitat on a given landscape, but embedded themselves in it, respecting the lay of the land.

In the American Southwest, the Anasazi people built adobe dwellings in south-facing cliff caves that took advantage of solar heat gain in the winter but blocked sun in summer. *Kivas*, or family units constructed partially underground, were fairly comfortable year-round, well-ventilated and relied on the enclosing earth for heating and cooling. The inhabitants often aggregated, then dispersed, moving into other homes or building new communities. In the thirteenth century the largest Anasazi communities peaked at between two thousand and twenty-five hundred people, the most the social structure and local resources could support.[1,2]

In Europe, climate changes after the last Ice Age caused tribes to move from southwest France and the Italian and Iberian peninsulas into northern regions. Relics of those civilizations, made of stone, a durable and easily preserved building material, have lasted to this day. Although the most famous sites are those thought to have ceremonial or burial purposes, such as Poulnabrone in western Ireland and Stonehenge in southern England, many buildings and entire villages indicate the prevalence of masonry construction.[3]

Skara Brae, which dates back to between 3100-2500 B.C., is a remarkably well preserved village on the Orkney Islands of Scotland consisting of stone houses with walls 10 feet (3 meters) high. The roofs were made of timber and whale ribs with an outer covering of living turf. Each home consisted of a single spacious room of about 388 square feet (36 square meters) with a hearth, furniture, including beds, shelves, and boxes made of stone. Excavation has shown that middens, or piles of domestic garbage, were used as building materials. Houses were constructed in pits in the midden, embedding them in a warm insulating material. During good weather, people lived atop, but retreated partially underground when the weather became rough.[4]

Subterranean homes were used in traditional towns and villages in the Chinese Loess Belt in the provinces of Hunnan, Shansi, and Kansu. Loess is easily carved sediment formed of silt that has been transported and deposited by the wind. The Chinese loess pits were about 1/8 acre (1/20 hectare) in area and 25-30 feet (7.6-9 meters) deep. Apartments of about 30 feet (9 meters) in depth and 15 feet (4.5 meters) in width were accessed through an L-shaped staircase from a central courtyard. Homes, schools, hotels, government offices and factories were built underneath fields, staying warm in the winter and cool in the summer.[5]

Cohabitating with nature and respecting human scale have always been the practice of the far north Inuit people. Such a principle is illustrated in the igloo, an archetypal building of Arctic regions, which arose as a migrating people faced harsh weather and had a single building material: snow. Its simple dome structure enclosed the largest volume for the smallest surface area, creating an extremely energy-efficient dwelling. Snow was cut into rectangular blocks that were stacked in a spiral fashion and finished with a key block on top, creating a self-supporting entity. The exit was made with a tunnel of snow blocks, small to reduce heat loss and below the main floor to passively encourage the exit of colder air. The structure often served as an overnight shelter. It could be added to in a radial pattern from the main room if more space and permanence were needed.[6]

Unlike Fargo's first settlers, the Inuit knew how to relate their dwellings, simple as they were, to the climate. The igloo's round aerodynamic shape let the strong winds fly over with little damage to the structure itself. Entryways were placed in consideration of wind directions and never faced north, and openings to let out stale air were punched in south-facing walls to take advantage of the sun. The aboriginal people, however, were nomadic tribes who changed campgrounds seasonally. When the snow melted, they moved to rich hunting and fishing grounds and housed themselves in different types of dwellings conforming to the local climate and environment.

The early settlers in North American winter cities seem to have neglected lessons that evolved over centuries in a trial-and-error process. What principles should have been followed? Perhaps the most rudimentary one has to do with wind. Lining up tall buildings along north-south axes should be avoided as it creates a tunnel effect. Walking in such streets is uncomfortable, and opening doors a struggle. When taller structures are proposed, the sides facing the prevailing wind direction should be stepped back to let the wind pass over them gently. Creating comfortable micro-climates is achieved by having taller buildings with unfenestrated northern walls which act as windbreaks to lower ones. This principle was used by Ralph Erskine, the Swedish architect and planner, in some of his Nordic communities' designs, notably in Svappavaara, a copper mining town in Sweden.

To avoid snow drifts, the piling-up of snow on the side of a building opposite to the wind direction, a round form and a roof with a low pitch should be used. When a rectangular building is to be constructed, the long axis has to be aligned parallel to the prevailing wind. The structure needs to be raised above ground to let wind carrying snow flow under it.

Where trees and bushes are present, they can help form a comfortable environment. Near bodies of water, like Fargo's Red River, wind commonly travels from the direction of the water towards the land in the daytime, but will reverse at night. Because of inertia, the wind flows around objects, and as a result, vegetation can greatly reduce the wind speed. During the cold months, coniferous trees, for example, shield buildings and people from northerly winter winds. Buildings, therefore, should be lower than the tree crowns. Such a practice lets homes benefit from south-eastern summer breezes; favorable positioning allows cross-ventilation and minimizes use of mechanical cooling means.

Despite fewer hours of sunlight in northern altitudes, designers can take advantage of the sun's free heat and light. Orienting the longest, most fenestrated facade to the south and giving the north elevation no, or smaller, openings will contribute to the occupants' comfort. Ensuring that tall buildings do not cast shadows on a long stretch of road will benefit pedestrians as well.

When the first European migrants arrived in the northern U.S. they altered the landscapes. An early step was the large-scale clearance of forest to create arable land, to produce building materials, and to use as a source of energy. The gradual disappearance of trees, unfortunately, transformed the natural micro-climate and allowed the wind to blow freely. The new settlers patterned the towns' layout of roads after models they knew best, the places from which they had come.

Once the wrong planning choices were made, they had to be compensated for by inventing other costly and foreign manmade solutions to shelter their inhabitants. One example of such a solution can be found in cities like Calgary, Winnipeg, and in Minneapolis, which I also visited on a cold winter day.

People were stepping off buses and hurrying into office towers that lined the street when I walked on Nicollette Street, one of Minneapolis' main thoroughfares. When I asked the hotel concierge where all the people were, he pointed toward an overhead skywalk connecting two buildings, handed me a map, and showed me how to get there. I strolled through an impressive web of skywalks connecting some thirteen city blocks in the north-south orientation and twelve along the east-west axis. The passageway links office towers with malls, hotels, the Target Centre public arena, the University of St. Thomas, and St. Olaf's Church. At this weekday-morning rush hour, the web was full of people, with some stopping at second-floor counters to grab a coffee on their way to work. At the end of each block, the passageway that ran through the buildings funnelled into glass tubes over the street traffic below. When I passed through again at midday, lunchtime crowds filled the meandering corridors. People walked, without coats, to their favorite restaurants blocks away, crossing through department stores with aisles of merchandise on either side.

The Minneapolis skywalks were introduced in the 1960s. The system expanded over the years to become an intricate network. Owners of new office towers need, it seems, to connect them to the web if they wish to attract tenants and patrons. I wondered about the system's impact on street-level activity. Did the skywalks draw pedestrians upwards to the detriment of life at ground level?

Large cities in the temperate zone have to grapple with the question of where to channel the flow of pedestrians.

Montreal, my home town, chose to build an underground network. The subway system, the Métro, was inaugurated just before the Expo 67 World's Fair began. The subway gave building owners and developers the opportunity to link buildings above and on either side to the subway. It was said that the mayor, Jean Drapeau, was against skywalks, fearing that they would switch off street-level life. As a result, Montreal got its enormous "underground city", which has turned into one of its notable tourist attractions. Was outdoor street-level action maintained? Not really. When winter cold strikes, for lack of appropriate outdoor design, pedestrians often prefer being indoors, either above or below ground. Given a choice of coming to a business via the street or through the system of indoor malls, in wintertime the choice is often to enter from the warm side.

Planning solutions for winter cities like Minneapolis and Montreal introduce a new urban paradigm. Fitting and attractive to citizens and visitors though these designs may be, they are artificial. Their builders attempted to combat nature rather than accommodate it. They eroded the inherent sense of place, or tried to invent a new one. Settlements whose very emergence is premised on ignoring nature, or imposing a new urban order, seem destined to have an unsustainable existence.

The attempt to ignore or alter nature is leading to a daunting prospect. Climate change and its attendant global warming are fast emerging as one of the greatest challenges to our existence. Polar icecaps are melting faster than ever, more and more land is being devastated by drought, and rising water levels are slowly threatening low-lying communities. One of the chief culprits is our poor urban practices. Constructing glass towers in northern cities, while ignoring wind directions, has led to increased consumption of non-renewable energy sources and the production of carbon dioxide that contributes to the greenhouse effect. The structures of these buildings must be strong enough to resist the wind, which consumes additional natural and economic resources. To reach these buildings from suburbia, still a major consideration even in this era of telecommuting, we have to accommodate ever-increasing vehicular traffic and pave over large tracts of fields and wind-blocking forest. This significantly raises summertime urban temperatures, increasing the demand for air conditioning in a vicious cycle.

AVI FRIEDMAN

I took a last look through the frigid air at Fargo's deserted Tenth Avenue, and then turned back and walked towards the comfort of my hotel, wondering what sense of place downtown Fargo could have had if only the first settlers had considered nature. I hope that proper considerations will be made in the design of future cities to benefit their inhabitants, visitors and the planet.

Ten

The Heart of York

THE SUN BROKE THROUGH GAPS in the gray clouds that hovered above York, England. It was early on a Saturday afternoon. John Wybor, my host, had invited me to join him and visit the city, whose history dates back to Roman, Anglo-Saxon, and Viking times. After spending two days in his architectural office, I was eager to see its famous cathedral and walk on the old walls.

Rain had made the gray stone slab pavement shiny all the way from Leeds, but it stopped just as we parked. We walked toward the town center through meandering, narrow streets lined with red brick, stone, and stucco-clad buildings. I kept looking up, amazed at how close the structure's tops were to each other. I could see a church tower. Typical of walled cities, the road pattern was chaotic.

The crowd thickened as we approached the center. Some walked in the opposite direction. They wore topcoats and held folded umbrellas as they carried bags with their purchases. Elderly men and women whispered into each other's ears, parents were trying to keep up with toddlers who rushed ahead, and young couples were holding hands.

From Aldwark Road we turned to St. Andrewgate, which took us into Church and Market streets where St. Sampson's and King's Squares meet to form a large open space. Measuring some 500 by 325 feet (150 by 100 meters), the place was framed by three- and four-story buildings of different styles, with a band of small stores on the bottom and apartments above. Among the upscale shops were several that provided the everyday food needs of the locals. They had equal-sized signage, some of it witty. Signs indicated that some of the upper floors were occupied by offices. Several cafés packed with late lunch-hour diners were tucked in between stores. There were empty outdoor tables, still wet, and no one was using them.

An open-air farmer's market with covered stalls lined one side. As I neared, I could see the busy vendors. They were exchanging greetings, handling their produce, and collecting money from patrons who they seemed to know. A band played music for adoring spectators, some of them dancing, on the opposite side of the square. Dressed in period costumes, a theater troupe performed in another section.

As I surveyed the entire scene, I wondered if I was witnessing a show staged for travelers from afar. The natural scene and the old buildings made it seem that if I were to roll back time, several centuries perhaps, the place would not change much. The square has aged gracefully and continues to welcome local residents and visitors who came to shop, see and be seen, meet, and get the local news.

I wondered why it all seemed so natural. Was it the place's proportions or the rustic buildings that framed it perhaps? Maybe it had to do with the people and activities, which reflected a sense of community. I began to question why civic squares are rarely included in the planning of contemporary neighborhoods. Is it a result of cultural and lifestyle changes? Are we less interested in meeting our fellow citizens? Do we have less in common to share? Have the digital media become the new people's square?

Open space devoted to public gatherings has formed an integral part of the urban and cultural heritage of many societies throughout history and played a critical role in the genesis of commerce, the emergence of democracy, and the vitality of civic life. Bearing different names, the square is known as the *plaza* in cities of Spanish origins, *piazza* in Italy, "village green" in settlements with feudal pasts, and "market squares" in others. The names all mean a physical clearance in the heart of a built place which can be of any shape— including square.

I wondered how squares came to be, in the evolution of cities and towns. Were they intentionally planned along with streets and residences, or were they leftover spaces, the afterthoughts of a build-ing process? Urban history demonstrates that both cases are true.

Similar to the emergence of present-day cities from former trading posts, military camps, or sprawling castles, which for various reasons expanded to become full-fledged communities, some squares were the outcome of accidental conditions. Others were purposely planned into a city's fabric, perhaps at the intersection of two arterial thoroughfares running perpendicular to each other. Yet other squares came to be when existing buildings were demol-ished or new ones erected. The square gained importance when one of the enclosing structures was a building of note such as a church, a temple, or the seat of a local ruler.

Squares evolved by accretion. Once defined, over time the place took on a life of its own. New buildings replaced old ones, dirt surfaces were paved, entry gates under which victorious armies might pass were erected, and monuments built in the center to mark special occasions or commemorate persons of note. In fact, squares distinguish themselves according to several features: the nature of the surrounding structures—their height, materials, and uses; the nature of their surface coverage; their location in and relation to the city's urban pattern, and their proportions, which determined their scale and affect the spatial impression by relating their height to their width and length.

Human scale affects a person's sense of place and comfort. A vast square, site of grand military parades and congregation of huge crowds, like Paris's Place de la Concorde, will feel bare when one stands alone in the empty middle. A smaller one will resonate as intimate, even friendly. Several "ideal" proportions have been proposed throughout history. The renowned planner Camilo Sitte suggested that the minimum dimensions a square ought to have would be equal to the height of the principal building on it; the maximum dimensions should not exceed twice that height.[1] Sitte's rule was based on a conviction that a person's line of vision should be between twenty-seven and forty-five degrees. Moughlin, a British planner, based on the recommendation of the Renaissance architect

Alberti Batista, suggested a proportion of one to six, since the viewing distance from the center easily permits enjoyment of all the
surrounding buildings.[2] Using this ratio, he suggested that each side
of a square surrounded by three-story buildings would be 180-230
feet (54-68 meters) long, and each side of a place with four-story
buildings would measure 240-300 feet (72-90 meters). There were
other features to distinguish one square from another, based on
their shapes.

In *Towns and Squares: from Agora to Village Green*, Paul Zucker
describes the basic types. The closed square, he argued, is the purest
of them all, the human quest for an orderly shape which can be a
perfect circle, square, or rectangle. Repetition of buildings with
equal height is a mark of such spaces, whose origins date back to
Hellenistic and Roman eras.[3]

A planning method which led to the creation of closed squares
and went on to inspire the design of numerous cities around the
world was developed by the ancient Greek architect and town
planner Hippodamus, when he designed the rebuilding of the Ionian
city of Miletus in 479 B.C. after it had been destroyed by the Persians.
Hoping to challenge the urban hegemony of Athens, with its well-
known Panathenaic Way, he developed a grid-plan system, where
the streets were uniform in width and the city blocks of equal
dimensions. The plan intentionally called for voids in the grid,
creating large public spaces around which important edifices were
constructed. The *agora*, located a short distance away from the port,
was the most prominent and included business and leisure centers
with access to a theatre, gymnasium, and stadium. A notable feature
of the place were the colonnades under an extended second story.
Known as *stoas*, they protected visitors from the elements and
provided display spaces outside stores for merchants. They offered
places for civility because while walking in the protected colonnade,
one might pause to talk with an acquaintance. Rome's Imperial
fora were made up of a series of closed squares, all connected to a
main thoroughfare.

Several European places were built in later centuries and

became prototypes of closed spaces. One was the Amfiteatro in the walled city of Lucca, Italy. It was constructed on the ruins of an ancient Roman amphitheater which had been destroyed during the barbarian invasions. It was designed in the seventeenth century by the architect Lorenzo Nottolini, who placed four- and five-story residences on top of the foundation's oval shape. It is a splendid example of an enclosed space with an open center. The row of stores and cafés that lines the lower floor makes it a gathering place for locals and tourists alike.

A square dominated by a notable feature, be it a building seen from one of its sides, an entry gate, or a central element such as a statue or a fountain, constitutes another type of space. One dates back to the sixth century B.C. The square in the Mesopotamian town of Babylon, present-day Iraq, was commissioned by Nebuchadnezzar II. Known for its hanging gardens, the city had processional routes connecting the massive Ishtar Gate to the square. It housed the Ziggurat, an eight-story pyramid-like structure, and a temple.[4,5]

Other squares with notable features were built in Europe centuries later. La Grande Place in Brussels, Belgium is a rectangular space, 360 by 220 feet (110 and 68 meters). It is dominated by the Gothic Town Hall with its elegant bell tower and, on the opposite side, a building known as the House of the King, which is surrounded by seventeenth-century guildhalls.

Many European squares have central features. One that stands out is Piazza Navona in Rome, which is fed by nine narrow streets. The square draws its form from the Circus Agonalis, a stadium which existed there in 91-96 A.D. A public market was built on top of the stadium's ruins. In 1648 the architect Bernini redesigned the space. He placed a broken obelisk, which was brought from the Appian Way, in the center. A sculpted fountain was built on the south side, and in 1878, the Fountain of Neptune was added at the north end. It is now one of the most visited places in the world.

The architectural historian Paul Zucker has coined a term "nuclear square" for a space of this sort, a central open area with one or more dominant features.[6] They were a feature of the Renaissance approach to the design of public spaces which was based on the study of perspective, the rules of geometry, and an appreciation of depth in space.[7] The view from each end was limitless. Many ended with a vista of a grand feature, such as a monu-mental building, obelisk, or arch. Such squares were the result of a distinct approach to town planning, especially when they were juxtaposed with broad boulevards lined with monuments. They were impressive in scale and stature, and yet they tended to be poorly regarded in relation to the everyday needs of the city's inhabitants. They lacked human scale and were not suited for small gatherings, open markets, or recreational activities. Nonetheless, in the centuries that followed, Renaissance-based master planning, with its nuclear squares, influenced the design of many of the world capitals which saw their fortunes rise after the Industrial Revolution.

Washington, D.C. was modeled after Renaissance planning principles. Its design included a number of nuclear squares. In 1791, Pierre Charles L'Enfant was appointed by President George Washington to design the new capital city. Combining principles of the Greek Milesian grid with a layout based on the design of several European capital cities, he set out to create a grandiose plan.[7] He introduced diagonal avenues connecting principal points such as the Capitol, the president's house, and the area which later became known as Lincoln Park. The final plan had twenty-four open squares, many of them visible from one another.

When several independent squares are placed in close proximity they are known as "grouped squares". The spaces may be of different sizes and forms, and each can have unique features, but they are linked and only separated by large buildings or other notable features. They may be the result of an unorderly evolutionary planning process as was the case in many European walled cities that left a number of open spaces once buildings were constructed. A prime example of such a sequence occurs in Venice. Walking through the city towards Piazza San Marco from almost any direction, one passes through expanded streets which function as squares. They are strung together to form a series of spaces, often with a structure such as a cistern or fountain at their center.

Zucker refers to "amorphous" squares. They may be any size, but they are odd-shaped, the result of prolonged urban trans-formations and planning conditions that saw large areas divided into leftover pieces of land, crossed by, or merged with, one or several streets. London's Trafalgar Square, with its off-center Nelson Column, New York's Times Square, the Plaça de la Palmera in Barcelona, and Boston's Post Office Square are examples.[8] In towns like Venice whose origins date back to the Middle Ages, however, such squares are smaller in scale.

The planning of towns and cities in the Middle Ages was influenced by their surrounding walls. Some, like Neubrandenburg in Germany, had a nuclear grid at first. In some cases, when the city expanded, a new perimeter with new protective walls was established and the old one was demolished to become a road, as is demon-strated in Milan, Italy. Other towns had a chaotic street order, such as may be seen to this day in Las Ramblas, Barcelona's old town. Both conditions created amorphous open spaces when roads crossed each other or met spaces which in later years evolved into something more formal. Some streets were widened, while in other cases buildings along one side were demolished to permit lateral expansion. Sometimes large openings were created at the town gate, or a void might be left in front of a cathedral or town hall; such is the case of many Tuscan towns. Those odd-shaped places are often marked by a central monument and they generally have a pleasant human scale.

Squares have made significant contributions to urban social and economic vitality. In *The City in History*, Lewis Mumford goes so far as to suggest that market squares are the most important invention of European city-making.[9] Trade practices, and their governance, began and flourished in these spaces. In larger towns, exchanges between merchants of different countries and heritage occurred, contributing to the evolution of cross-border commerce.

In the *Wisdom of Cities*, Suzanne H. Crowhurst Lennard and

Henry L. Lennard argue that "the square provides an unparalleled school for social learning, for exercise of responsibility and for the development of a sense of community and democratic decision-making."[10] Creating an outdoor living room for citizens to meet face-to-face was instrumental in fostering a web of relationships and communal security. Children congregated there to play and adults for various purposes.

From ancient times, squares were the cradles of democratic forms of government. Representatives might be elected there, and the town hall, a symbol of local order, was built there. Squares in front of cathedrals radiated spirituality. Visual links to the past through commemorative monuments were a daily reminder of local history. Statues recognized the contributions of personages to politics, culture, art, or science. Squares played an important role in maintaining traditions. Military parades celebrated important victories or national holidays. Squares were the scene of religious processions or sports competitions such as the famous Palio horse race in the Piazza del Campo in Siena. People often resided in the buildings that framed squares, commonly above ground-floor businesses. The mix of uses and the constant presence of people who lived on the square, or who came to shop or visit, softened the built landscape.

The square's place in urban history began to change in the aftermath of the Industrial Revolution. The British residential squares, their rise and evolution, manifest this transition in town planning. Many squares that were open plazas in the seventeenth century were enclosed as private parks at the end of the eighteenth century, based on the social values of the aristocracy, which were later adopted by the middle class.[11] The squares, with their rural-like landscapes, were closed to the general public to express a desire for class segregation, residential isolation, and privatization of open space—principles which decades later would be the foundations of suburban living.

Seventeenth-century squares and the residences that surrounded them were owned by a single landowner. Local residents and the general public had access to all public spaces. In the following century, people purchased their homes, and introduced a new measure to control the use of squares; not much different than today's condominium law, this restricted access to the public areas to residents only, and permitted collection of improvement fees from each homeowner. It was a bold move away from the feudal system to individual rights. The square's landscaping had a rural, scenic connotation which conveyed a desire to enjoy country life in the city. Such squares were conceived as stand-alone spaces with homes permitting a view of the comings and goings.

The designers of these residential squares introduced architectural uniformity based on strict interpretation of Palladian rules.[12] As city centers became crowded, and polluted, estates were constructed on the outskirts of large metropolitan areas. A good example of both can be found in Bath, where John Wood, Sr. and his son built the Queen's Square in 1732, the King's Circus in 1754, and the Royal Crescent in 1767.[13] Designed at first as resort communities, they went on to become a harbinger of what was to happen in following centuries: the turning of vacation enclaves into full-fledged suburban towns reached by rail and later by automobile. Houses soon featured a backyard which was often turned into a garden.[14] The public area became more secluded and off-limits to non-residents. Commercial features, such as shops and markets, were not included. These moves suited the social values of the rising middle class that grew in size in the aftermath of the Industrial Revolution.

The century that followed saw a rise in the popularity and the further establishment of suburban ideals and planning concepts. Smaller, lower-cost dwellings made home ownership in towns on the periphery of large metropolitan areas accessible to many. New planning principles, distinct from urban ones, emerged and the common Milesian grid system was abandoned in favor of new ideas.

In North America, where the design of suburban communities flourished shortly after it did in Europe, some developments were planned by landscape architects who introduced free-flowing, curved, tree-lined streets; an example is Riverside, Illinois, designed by Olmsted, Vaux and Company.[15] New street patterns, such as loop roads and cul-de-sacs, offered safety and tranquility. Some green space was part of each individual lot, in front and at the rear of the house. The public square became a casualty of suburban planning.

The advantages of traditional urban squares were not possible to achieve in suburban settings. Their design rarely called for such places, as the low population density could not support much commerce even under apartments, and a configuration of detached low-rise dwellings was inadequate to frame a space to begin with. Golf courses, public parks, and shopping malls were meant to be the new village green. Unfortunately, none of these amenities could replace the social web, face-to-face encounters, mixes of ages, and the cultural symbolic value of squares. Subdivisions were robbed of a fundamental civility and community-building feature.

Suburban developments dealt a blow to traditional urban hubs. Commerce followed the migration of citizens to the periphery. Author Arthur Frommer argues that "[t]he extinction of America's down-towns has occurred all over the country as a direct result of mall development on the outskirts, and especially because of the construction there of mammoth stores of the Wal-Mart variety. In addition to disfiguring those outskirts, they have forced out of business nearly every major category of downtown shop."[16]

In advance of a proposed 100,000-square-foot (9,300-square-meter) big-box development in St. Albans, Vermont, an impact assessment study estimated that it would cost the public three dollars for every dollar of public benefit. The proposal was rejected.[1] Shopping malls and, later, retail parks known as power centers, with their off-the-shelf designs in the middle of huge parking lots were meant to offer alternatives to squares. They were poor replacements, drawing people, who did not know each other, from afar and creating artificial environments centered around consumption.

New social attitudes, lifestyle trends, and technological innovation influenced the demise of the square in urban planning. Public gatherings were once the means of information exchange through

word of mouth, public announcements, and posters. The rise of
the print and later of electronic media made it unnecessary to walk
to the town center to find out what was going on. Cyberspace
became the new public square through social networking programs
such as Facebook and MySpace, with sixty-four million and eighteen
million visitors respectively in April 2007.[18]

Can we make civic squares relevant again? Can they play a role
in our urban and social lives? Rolling back time hardly works in
planning and architecture because it simply fosters imitations, often
grotesque in character. What we can do, however, is revive forgotten,
once-flourishing downtowns with their beautiful squares. It is not
hopeless; there are recent examples of civic squares that have become
an important anchor in North America's urban renewal projects.
To make themselves livable places, some cities, like Minneapolis,
have built hockey arenas and ballparks in the downtown core; others
have opened farmers' markets in squares. And so it was that, during
the 1990s, older cities like Seattle and Chicago were revived. Living
downtown in new or converted industrial buildings next to cultural
and shopping amenities became fashionable, and followed the
emergence of non-traditional households. Many singles, young
couples, and elderly people have made city living their choice. There
are cases where the quest for alternatives to suburban sub-divisions,
based on old town-planning traditions, has led to the design of
communities with squares at their hearts. These squares are, in turn,
framed by row housing with a mix of commercial and public
amenities within walking distance of all edges of the neigh-borhood,
demonstrating that squares can, once again, become vibrant parts
of new towns.

Standing in the heart of York's main square, watching the
crowds passing by, made me recognize that some trends, urban
included, may come and go, as history renders them obsolete. Others
hold vital roles and should never be let go, even if interest in them
declines for a while. Squares are places where hidden social bonds
can be felt and, therefore, efforts to conserve or bring them back
are well deserved.

Eleven

The Kitchen of Pina and Felice

THE VIEW FROM PINA AND FELICE'S KITCHEN was breathtaking. The Tuscan hills, some covered with freshly-cut light yellow hay, rolled on gently into the horizon. I could see rows of green grapevines hanging from wires, and patches of sunflowers and olive groves dotting the natural quilt. On distant hilltops, I could spot homes with red terracotta roof tiles, just like the one in which we were sitting.

A large uncovered wooden table occupied the center of the room. Pots and pans hung over a counter covered with fresh produce ready for a meal. A cross was affixed above a passageway; at its end I saw a bedroom with a large bed. White linens and pillows rested on a windowsill to be freshened by the morning's gentle sun. Our voices echoed off the ceramic floor tiles and the white plaster walls. Pina served coffee and told me that they had moved here from the Island of Sardinia in southern Italy about twenty years ago. Unable to find land in their own birthplace, they purchased this farm where they invested the better years of their lives. Noticing heavy tourist traffic en route to the nearby town of Volterra, they wanted to supplement their income by joining the hospitality business. In addition to farming, they now had five rental suites, including the one in which I was staying.

She and her husband Felice recalled how challenging it had been to convert some of the rooms of their farm's main building into *Agroturismo*. In Tuscany, Felice explained, new construction in the countryside is strictly forbidden. Locals are only permitted to renovate or add to existing structures. The provincial authority,

Pina added, had recognized that the beauty of the countryside would not last if rapid development took place. To obtain a permit, they had to engage a certified restoration expert, who measured and drew meticulous drawings of their seventeenth-century building. They had considered constructing a small dining room, but were refused, she said.

As I sipped the strong aromatic coffee, I looked at the scene outside and realized that this landscape had been cultivated for centuries and that it had molded, one could say, the people who labored in it. If the strict laws were to be lifted, probably the old buildings would be demolished and the land use rapidly changed from agricultural to commercial or residential. The landscape would be paved over. Low-density gated condominium estates for wealthy overseas investors would likely follow. Roads would be expanded to accommodate an increased traffic flow, shopping malls and big box stores would be built. Ignoring preservation, the Tuscans realized, would not only erase architectural heritage and alter the landscape, but would uproot a way of life that has lasted centuries.

What, then, do people who wish to build do? I asked. They either divide an existing dwelling to make room for a newlywed family member, or move to a part of Tuscany or elsewhere in Italy where land is still available and construction of new buildings is permitted. This usually means moving to a city. As Felice explained this, I wondered whether these measures were not too harsh. Why are the Tuscans keen on preserving the past, apparently at the expense of their future? Why has meticulous attention to old buildings become so important? How can one decide what is worth preserving? Will our contemporary buildings, mediocre as they may be, become tomorrow's heritage? Do cultivated landscapes constitute a heritage? And how important is heritage, with its many faces, to the creation of sense of place?

The conviction that old buildings should be preserved has evolved through successive eras. Historically, people perceived ancient structures as reflections of human continuity, an enduring extension of the past, and symbols to be retained. In the first century B.C.,

Roman architect Marcus Vitruvius Pollio compiled a manual of guiding principles for building and maintenance practices. *De Architectura* introduced guidelines aimed at ensuring that new structures would be harmoniously integrated with existing ones. The manual emphasized that appropriate design depended on the education of the architect. Vitruvius argued that without an extensive knowledge of history, designers would lose the symbolic meaning of urban and architectural elements.[1] Harmony among edifices, it was suggested, created a simultaneous sense of continuity that defined a place.[2]

Vitruvius's legacy inspired the Roman emperors Valentinian and Valerius who, four hundred years later, began the restoration of Rome. The two rulers rehabilitated the city's dilapidated Forum and restored dignity to public buildings. They not only conserved historically significant structures, but restored their former uses. In the eighth century, medieval leaders such as Charlemagne sought to reinstate classical architectural traditions, and by the fifteenth century a civic consciousness of such magnitude emerged that cities like Florence and Siena competed to become cultural hubs by building to high artistic standards specifically to create a future legacy. The buildings around the Piazza del Campo in Siena, for example, were designed according to guidelines established in 1297 that have been respected to the present day.[3]

The eighteenth-century Enlightenment brought forward new scientific, spiritual, economic, and political ideas. The notion of history changed as it moved towards scientific inquiry which disassociated past from present. The emphasis on historic preservation, however, was not maintained. The Romantic movement of the nineteenth century spurred an ideology of stewardship, which recognized that a balance could exist between progress and past events. The notion of "custodianship" evolved, which implied civic responsibility toward the built heritage.[4] Custodianship, however, regarded heritage in isolation from contemporary building activity, and the built heritage was rarely integrated into new design ideas. The relatively few buildings that were conserved often stood alone.

A similar approach was represented by Berthault's 1812 plan for the Roman Forum archaeological area. Ancient monuments became the focal points of the scheme, with the rest ignoring the old.

The nineteenth-century Stylistic Restoration movement aspired to make use of and preserve old architectural elements. Some old buildings regained their economic importance, and restoration with an eye to an aesthetic unity increased an area's prestige. In tune with the economic climates that defined the nineteeenth and twentieth centuries, private initiatives helped create and capitalize on a new market niche. Simply put, entrepreneurs discovered that history could be sold.[5,6]

Post-World War II technological advancements, economic affluence, and generous fiscal housing policies had a dominant influence on urban development. Respect for historic harmony was largely ignored, and attention was directed to the construction of mass-produced new projects rather than the renovation of old ones. The last century saw the rise of the Modern movement as an ideological reaction to nineteenth-century design that emphasized efficiency.[7] The International Style emphasized buildings with exposed concrete, steel, and glass, bearing no resemblance to old structures. Designers failed to take advantage of the richness that the surrounding old buildings provided, in favor of a fresh start.

How should we regard our old buildings? Should all municipal legislators be strict like the Tuscans, prohibiting any change, or should we permit exterior or interior adaptation to contemporary uses and technologies?

Several strategies have been introduced to reconcile modern development with heritage preservation. The conservationist view sees proper preservation of historical buildings as windows on past societies. Much like the Tuscan belief, this view encourages strict preservation so that the buildings may serve not only an educational purpose, but also provide a certain sense of place, rooted in history. A functionalist view, on the other hand, mediates heritage conflicts that arise between economic and cultural values. It considers that buildings must be functional while being historically respectful.[8]

For example, the structures adjacent to the historic Ponte Vecchio over the river Arno in Florence were rebuilt using modern techniques after the devastation of World War II. The style of the new buildings and the relationships among them, however, kept the same rhythm and volume as those designed centuries earlier.

The "sense of place" perspective on heritage combines the two preceding principles of preservation: uniformity and relationship. Instead of focusing on specific buildings, this view looks at the unique qualities of a community as a whole. In other words, attractive communities are organic when they develop upon evolving social and built foundations. The significance of the sense of place view is evident in trends extending historic building legislation to the protection of entire areas. This reflects a growing awareness that stand-alone old buildings lose meaning when isolated among modern structures.[9] Therefore, greater value is created by edifices that are related to each other by replicating the style of old buildings. New structures in Venice, Italy, for example, are built upon old heritage traditions to ensure that a sense of place is harmoniously maintained and to reflect the city's historic identity. Continuous conservation, which pays attention to large and small architectural details, has resulted in maintaining a distinctive sense of place.

One North American city which has retained its unique appearance through conservation efforts is San Francisco, where early nineteenth-century townhouses with colorful facades have kept their charm despite being in the shadow of tall modern buildings. The city is known for the active interest that its citizens take in preserving their built environment. Alamo Square demonstrates the city's efforts. The Square has maintained an architectural harmony through many phases of development. This sense of continuity was dependent on the recognition that a new design tradition can be developed within the framework of existing buildings, and changes in Alamo Square occurred slowly. Moreover, the recognition of a building's historical value allowed contemporary designers to both preserve and innovate using traditional features, which resulted in a distinct sense of place. Perhaps more than most American cities,

San Francisco's planners have realized that heritage is essential to maintaining a quality urban fabric. In 1978 the city introduced a strict planning code to guide new development according to principles of heritage continuity.[10]

Another sensible example of urban renewal that interweaves new and old occurred in Birmingham, England. Lying northwest of England's second largest city center, the Birmingham Jewellery Quarter boasts a two-hundred-year-old identity from the industrial era that shaped much of Birmingham's built landscape. The urban form consisted primarily of three-story nineteenth-century brick buildings that housed small factories, workshops, and families. The middle-class population which inhabited the area until the 1950s, was displaced as war damage and safety concerns condemned many old structures. Successive 1960s planning visions cleared other areas in favor of massive block redevelopment, but not the Jewellery Quarter. As a result, the district remained undeveloped.[11]

A combination of events sparked interest in the city's architectural history as a backlash to modernity. The local Victorian Society lobbied city officials to enact conservation legislation for the historic quarter. Through careful documentation of old structures, the society introduced strict regulations with the support of the city planning department. In 1980, Birmingham City Council legislated protection of the unique character of the Jewellery Quarter. Demolition of old buildings and new development were prohibited and restoration was encouraged. Both private and public funding stimulated revitalization within the delineated area. The adaptive reuse of former workshops as commercial spaces reflected an awareness of the complex relationship between heritage and economic values. As a result, locals, homeowners, businesses, and tourists have moved back into the now-thriving quarter.

What, then, constitutes a heritage building? It is an expert's domain that, in a number of cities, has become a highly debatable and charged topic.

The question of what will constitute tomorrow's historic buildings is even more relevant. Years from now, will glass office towers be considered worth preserving? Will someone shed a tear if a 1960s surburban bungalow is demolished? Can a big box store built on the outskirts of town be considered heritage?

Buildings from centuries past are reflections of the care and craftsmanship that their architects, builders, and craftsmen took in designing and erecting them. Upscale or modest residences, institutional buildings or factories all seem to have cherished and admired features. Stained glass windows, intricate façade brickwork, unique ironwork on a guardrail or elevator doors, exquisite stone arrangement, and imaginative woodwork are hallmarks of past eras. Paying attention and investing in details was possible in a time of low labor and material costs, and few building booms. Simple, modest structures were built, yet even in them there was an attempt to fit the structure in with its surroundings and to respect an urban context.

Some modern architects introduced beautifully expressed simplicity and cleanliness of forms, for example Le Corbusier's 1931 Villa Savoye or Walter Gropius's 1926 Bauhaus building. The same language was expressed in the interior and furniture designs and was a truly refreshing style when it was first introduced. Early modern buildings offered novelty, whereas many builders of later structures simply took advantage of the simplicity that the style offered. Speculative buildings altered our sense of place by introducing repetition and sameness to cities.

Well-crafted old buildings from centuries past need to be appreciated not only as *objets d'art*, but as place-creating tools and ongoing manifestations of who we are. Cultivated farm landscapes should be considered for their heritage value. Tuscany's past and culture are linked to winemaking and olive harvesting, which constitute the livelihood of older generations of farmers and future ones who may wish to follow in their footsteps. Vineyards, olive groves, and patches of sunflowers created Tuscany's most recognizable sense of place, and are therefore justifiably preserved.

Looking through Pina and Felice's kitchen door into the distance, I realized that centuries-long commitments are necessary to preserve buildings, create architectural and landscape heritage, and unique places. The Tuscans turned their province into what it has become: a beautiful countryside that attracts visitors from afar. It has already paid off and the tourist dollars are pouring in as the land is being preserved. They selected the route of self-imposed discipline that is appreciated now and will be valued more in years to come.

Twelve

Pathways in Kfar Sava

~

I TOOK A LEISURELY STROLL THROUGH the streets of Kfar Sava, enjoying the bright, warm December sun. In a few days I would return home and brave a Canadian winter. The Israeli town, population seventy-six thousand, is located in the Sharon region, in the eastern central part of the country. Four- to six-story white stucco-clad apartment buildings line the streets. The upper floors are terraced back, balconies are crowded with plants, and cars park under an elevated second story.

A sign pointing to a *simta* (lane) caught my eye. The paved 10-foot (3-meter) wide passageway ran between tall buildings. Orange trees grew on one side and streetlights with glass globes were installed intermittently along on the other. After a short walk along the lane, I crossed Herzl Street and then I entered a square park, framed by apartment buildings, with a small play structure and tall broadleaf trees in its center. People stood on some of the upper-story balconies, watching children at play below. Two Russian-speaking men sat on a bench and whispered in each other's ears. Three young women occupying another bench facing the play area spoke with bold hand gestures, pausing from time to time to gently shake a stroller or shout at a child. There was something natural, even pastoral, in the tableau. The trees, the sounds, the conversations, and the sun added a warm backdrop to the setting.

I continued my walk, nodding to a passerby carrying bags full of groceries. He seemed to have arrived from Rothschild Street, a busy artery that one could reach via the path. Patrons walked in and out of a grocery and a hardware store on the lower floor of a building. I crossed the road and walked into the next cluster. Tall trees, a man-made grassy hill, and a play structure to which several toddlers clung formed its heart. The path took me to a pedestrian mall where people sat around tables under arched colonnades in Café Mango. A beautifully landscaped civic square with a performing arts center and a library lay in the distance.

I arrived at Kenyon Arim, Kfar Sava's main open-air shopping mall. The fashionable stores on various levels were crowded and many people sat at the ground floor cafés, warming in the sun. The residences above the stores had staggered balconies. I could see people watching the commotion below.

It had taken fifteen minutes to traverse the six-block stretch, a pleasant stroll in a town of neighborhoods. The path, an urban artery of a sort, connected edges, offered opportunities to turn a stranger into an acquaintance, and to get a bit of exercise. But what I found even more important was the way it enabled me to see a place and know its culture. Walking in Kfar Sava, I experienced intimacy with people and proximity to objects that I could not have had in a car. I could view details and read expressions because of the slow rhythm in which the information revealed itself.

Walking, I reflected, is a necessary instrument for the appreciation of a place. We, unfortunately, are not doing much of it today, and, as a result, we compromise our ability to connect and know and have a better sense of place.

In fact, over the past half century North Americans have progressively diminished the amount of walking they do in a day. A long or short walk to a friend's house, a corner store, a library, or a school has been replaced by a ride. A survey of Canadian municipalities found that many did not provide pedestrian amenities at all, and only half, in any way, encouraged their citizens to reach their destinations by foot.

Is walking related to people's place of residence? It certainly is. Whereas urban dwellers tend to walk more, living in a sparsely populated suburban area increases our dependence on the car. With mushrooming urban sprawl, the distance between homes and most other destinations has widened. Only 14 percent of Canadians report living within a 1.5 mile (2.5 km) walking distance of work. Of those, 49 percent never walk. On a typical weekday, for example, 75 percent of all adults commute to work by car. Commuting time per person now stands at an average of 58 minutes per day.[1] It frightens me to think that people who reside in suburban or rural towns may spend three to five years of their lives driving, time that could have been spent with family or on leisure activities.

Why are we walking less? Have our driving habits eroded our sense of place? The answer is rooted in urban transformations, in particular those that occurred in the past half century. A long step back to an ancient town that has maintained its walkability is a good place to start.

European medieval cities had many features that made them walkable. They were smaller than their classical predecessors, and work and home were often combined, so the entire city had a small footprint and its edges were within easy reach. Dubrovnik, a thriving city in present-day Croatia, is an example of such a settlement. Concentrated at the harborfront, the city center links a series of squares into one another through narrow streets and dense structures. Key government or ecclesiatical buildings dominate some squares, while monuments are featured in the center of others. In a typical old building there is a store or a workshop on the ground floor, a reception room on the second, and a family living space on the third.

A telling example of how compact and walkable Dubrovnik is can be found in Norbert Schoenauer's book *6000 Years of Housing*.[2] He noted that the city's area, 40 acres (16 hectares), houses five thousand people in about two thousand dwellings. There are twenty-six churches or chapels, a synagogue, a mosque, two monasteries, a convent, and a college. There are scores of shops, workshops, and restaurants, one indoor and two outdoor theaters, a few museums, a palace, a city hall, a customs house, a mint, a granary and an active harbor. Yet with all these amenities, the city is spread over an area equivalent in size to *one* cloverleaf intersection of a typical American interstate highway! Dubrovnik has remained livable for centuries. Cars cannot pass through many streets to this day.

European urban planning changed dramatically during the Renaissance. The organic development characteristic of medieval cities like Dubrovnik diminished with the separation of work and home. Then as the Industrial Revolution increased production rates to unprecedented levels and concentrated it in cities, there was a massive rural-to-urban migration of people in search of employment. People lived in appalling conditions due to overcrowding and poor sanitation.

The squalor planted the seed of change and the desire in the minds of some to see neighborhoods become healthier living spaces. In 1898, British planner Ebenezer Howard published *Garden Cities of Tomorrow*. He proposed a circular city, with industry located at the town center, surrounded by a ring of parkland. Around the park was a crystal palace, a glass arcade for shopping. The next ring consisted of private houses with attached gardens. These were enclosed by a broad avenue, which separated the residential from the industrial areas. At the periphery were rail lines and then farms. It was a walkable concept with access between and across the rings. Howard's Garden City concept was first implemented in the town of Letchworth, England, north of London. In 1903, the Garden City Pioneer Company bought 1,529 hectares (3,822 acres) of land and hired Raymond Unwin and Barry Parker to translate Howard's diagram for the site. The town's form was made of a number of squares surrounded by housing. The squares were connected to one another via short streets and pathways, all leading to a main square.[3,4]

Radburn, New Jersey is a renowned product of collaboration between planners Clarence Stein and Henry Wright, built in 1920. It is based on a translation to North America of principles espoused by Howard and put into practice by Unwin and Parker. Among its many innovations, the scheme, for the first time, accommodated the automobile and separated pedestrian and vehicular traffic via interior paths and overpasses. The boldest characteristic of the plan was the use of cul-de-sacs, a feature which would be widely emulated in later years. Zoning, which was introduced across North America's urban centers in the 1920s, separated large swathes of Radburn's residential areas from all other land uses. Created to simplify development processes, zoning formally distinguished home and work, and increased the distances to be traveled by car, diminishing walking.[5]

The early decades of the twentieth century set the stage for what was about to occur in mid-century. Housing shortages in cities after World War II, the availability of plenty of cheap land, the affordability of automobiles, and the development of mass construction techniques combined to foster the emergence of suburbia. Levittown, North America's first large-scale planned suburb, was constructed on former Long Island potato fields. The Levitt Corporation originally planned two thousand units in 1947, but by the end of the year the project expanded by a whopping six thousand additional units.[6,7]

Low density, vast distances, wide roads, and avoidance of commerce in the town center all made walking to most destinations impossible. Lanes, a valuable link that fostered walking in older communities, vanished with the proliferation of suburban planning. Lanes were a prominent feature in cities and neighborhoods until half a century ago. In the horse and buggy era, their role was primarily utilitarian: to provide rear access for a stable and for deliveries of coal or heating oil, firewood, and milk, for example, as well as garbage collection. The paved, often lit, surfaces served as improvised basketball courts with hoops over rear garages. From a rear kitchen window or a back porch, parents would watch their kids play safely.

With the introduction of municipal utility connections to the fronts of properites and the elimination of home deliveries, lanes gradually lost their appeal. Cities began to pay greater attention to house fronts and soon discovered that money could be saved by not building lanes at all. The lane began to disappear, and with it citizens lost a safe secondary pedestrian network that served an important social role. Fences began to surround homes, preventing easy crossing of a city block to reach a neighboring house or play area. The dynamics of knowing a place through walking in alleys no longer existed.

Planning decisions regarding school locations in suburban areas affected the walking habits of children. Due to their low density, several neighborhoods had to share a school. It meant that in most developments the distance between home and school grew significantly. In Canada, studies show that only 37 percent of 5- to 13-year-olds and 33 percent of 14- to 18-year-olds walk to school. Only 2 percent and 4 percent of those respective age groups cycle, although most children have access to a bicycle. Decreased accessibility, such as longer distance to neighborhood schools, was cited by 53 percent of those youngsters' parents as barriers to walking.[8]

Not surprisingly, about half of all walking activities occur in the home itself, while the remainder occur an average of 10 miles (16 kilometers) away from home. Fewer than 30 percent of trips are within the range usually associated with one's immediate community, which is less than 5 miles (8 kilometres). People drive an average of 10.7 miles (17.2 kilometers) for social and recreational activities and 7.7 miles (12.4 kilometers) to shop.[7] The average time reported spent in cars by women now stands at 64 minutes daily.

Does the diminished amount of walking affect health? It certainly does. According to *Overweight and Obesity in Canada: A Population Health Perspective*, a report by Kim Raine, the total daily energy expenditure is the sum of the resting metabolic rate plus the thermal effect of food (obligatory energy expenditure) plus energy expended in physical activity. Any significant decrease in daily energy expenditure contributes to rising rates of obesity. It is simply a vicious circle.

In a study associating "sprawl indices" of U.S. counties and metropolitan areas with health data from the 1998-2000 Behavioral Risk Factor Surveillance System, living in a sprawling county was associated with less walking. A 2005 survey by the Canadian Heart and Stroke Foundation found that 80 percent of Canadians believe that city living and its high pressure, fast-paced lifestyle are detrimental to health. But according to the foundation, for people in the suburbs, smaller towns, and rural areas, a false sense of security could be putting them at higher risk of heart disease and stroke than their city-dwelling counterparts. The Foundation's research shows that city dwellers are twice as likely to walk, cycle, or take public transit to work as their non-urban citizens. In addition, more urban folks walk or bike to destinations of daily chores.

The rapid increase of obesity among North Americans is due to poor dietary choices and sedentary lifestyle. In 2000-2001, more than six million Canadian adults aged 20 to 64 were overweight and nearly three million were obese, an increase of over two-and-a-half times over the past two decades. Studies have shown that each additional kilometer walked per day reduces the likelihood of becoming obese by nearly 5 percent, while each hour per day spent in a car increases the likelihood of becoming obese by 6 percent.[1]

The rate of increase of obesity among children is particularly troubling. In the past three decades in Canada, obesity rates in children have almost tripled. Because of the health implications, the World Health Organization is now regarding obesity as a global epidemic requiring immediate action. A 1999 article in *The New England Journal of Medicine* suggests that overweight and obese people increase their risk of cardiovascular illnesses by four times. They run a fivefold risk of diabetes, and have greater risk of hypertension, gallbladder disease, and certain cancers. The author suggests that the overall risk of mortality increases by two and a half times.[9] The decline of walking has altered our sense of place as well.

How can we design new communities, and modify older ones, to encourage pedestrians? In the past half-century, municipal planners pretty much eliminated walking routes and destinations from neighborhoods. They should reverse course and reintroduce them.

In a talk to the American Transportation Research Board, Dan Burden, director of the Orlando-based Walkable Communities, Inc., outlined several principles worth considering.[10] Citing Portland,

Oregon as an example of a successful walkable city, Burden suggested that affordable and reliable public transportation that reaches across neighbourhoods and links them to city centers can "unchain people from car keys". Using the term "walking scale", Burden argues that towns and neighborhoods can be planned from the outset with walkers in mind. Location of commercial and institutional buildings need not exceed a comfortable ten-minute walk from home. Once the location of a community's public functions has been determined, a network of pathways can link them to one another and to the residences. To make walking efficient and safe, short blocks are preferable; cars slow down when they approach an intersection. To keep speed and volume of cars low, the number and lanes can be reduced, street width can be shrunk, and the road surface changed from asphalt to interlocking concrete pavers. Burden suggests that roads should have multiple uses because this "can elicit appropriate behavior and increase neighborliness, association, belonging, acceptance, pride, and play." When a street intersects a pathway, it should be easy to cross on foot.

Sidewalks should not be too narrow. There should be a buffer between the sidewalk and the road, and sidewalks should be well-maintained year-round. Icy sidewalks will keep walkers, primarily the elderly, indoors in wintertime. They need to be cleaned of snow and ice. Sidewalks should be landscaped with trees. With landscaping and a buffer, they are comfortable and safer to walk on. Trees can shade benches along the sidewalk, and they create a pleasant sound when the breeze blows through them. The design of sidewalks and pathways must foresee all users. Parents pushing strollers, the elderly with walkers, and wheelchair users should all be comfortable. The number of interruptions to the continuity of a sidewalk, and in particular cut-offs by driveways, should be minimal.

Open green spaces and areas for public functions which have been stripped from neighborhoods need to be designed back into them. The "culture of big", which has seen power centers render mom-and-pop stores unprofitable, and has amalgamated small play areas into large fields far from most houses, should be reviewed.

Destinations that are a walking distance away need to be reintro-
duced. Local multifunctional destinations can be viewed as social
generators and magnets, places to meet a neighbor or make a new
acquaintance. Zoning bylaws need to be altered. They should be
based on the principle of fostering a sense of place.

Can we turn neighborhoods into walkable places again? Oh,
yes. We need to retool our minds and change personal and communal attitudes and habits. Walking should be regarded as a natural
function. It creates interaction between people. It fosters relations
among neighbors and enhances fitness. The well-being of humans
needs to take priority over accommodating vehicular traffic. By
planning with these considerations in mind, we stand a greater
chance of introducing places that are engaging and livable.

Thirteen

London's Humility

I STEPPED INTO LONDON'S MISTY MORNING to walk around
Kensington, where my hotel was located. It had rained the night
before and the streets were fresh. A hesitant winter sun broke
through the thick gray clouds above. Red double-decker buses
passed by, stopped at the corner, and let off children in gray school
uniforms. Shopkeepers unlocked front doors and posted signs to
welcome patrons. I ventured into a side road, lined with rows of
identical white stucco-clad townhouses. Stairs under a second-floor
terrace held up by columns led into each house. A black cast-iron
fence marked the boundary between private and public domains.

Through a gap in the rows, I noticed a cobblestone-paved mews,
a court framed by low-rise buildings that in older times had housed
horses and carriages, and which had been converted into residences.
Built of gray limestone, the structures in the mews looked as though
they had been constructed in different periods, yet they all had
roughly the same height, materials, and even window proportions.
Front entrances, part of a former larger opening, were painted in a
variety of colors to lend identity. Window sills and doorways had
flowerpots on or next to them. I continued my walk and entered a
small park with paved pathways, play structures, shrubs, and mature
leafy trees that cast shadows on benches underneath. Everything fit
together nicely.

Looking around at the park, the homes in the mews and the
townhouses in the distance, I wondered what made it a pleasant,
complete urban scene? I could recall one aspect: cohesion. There was
no visual competition between the homes in the row on the main
street, the signage on storefronts, the buildings in the mews, or

even the trees in the park. Nothing screamed for attention. It seems that someone had blessed the place and its designers with humility. I had no doubt that at some point, London had put in place bylaws to respect this order. Yet, it felt that a self-governing discipline, rather than an imposition from above, had choreographed the ensemble.

Reflecting on typical contemporary suburban communities, I wondered why humility is in short supply nowadays. Why do so many developers and homeowners embrace a "show-off," sometimes vulgar attitude with multiple building heights, odd shapes of roofs, various window sizes and types, and a range of exterior materials—all on the same street? Is it a reflection of a quest to express individuality, or maybe social status? Are we, by doing so, compromising a sense of place, or not giving it a chance to emerge? Is cohesion necessary to create a beautiful place? Can it be imposed by stringent control mechanisms such as zoning bylaws?

London, in fact, set milestones in the evolution of architectural controls. Such controls, historians suggest, date back to Babylon and the famous Code of Hammurabi, its ruler in the seventh century B.C., as well as to Greek and Roman planners. In 1666, following the devastation caused by the Great Fire of London, controls were introduced to regulate construction. The rules were meant to ensure safety; they discouraged use of flammable materials like timber in favor of masonry. The regulations mandated uniform facades and a fixed number of floors.[1]

The rapid urban growth that occurred during the Industrial Revolution brought with it an increase in land speculation. In addition to guarding public safety, architectural controls regulated the appearance of buildings, streets, and neighborhoods and thereby helped developers attract desired clients and discourage others. A minimum quality of construction, specific building materials, and minimal ceiling, window, and railing heights were often dictated by these codes as well.[2]

Neighborhood character and appearance were seen as essential to maintain and increase property value. The Royal Crescent Estate at Bath, near London, built in 1769, is an early example of this type of control. Lots were leased rather than sold to give the developers control over the final form of each building. By including elevation drawings in the contractual building agreements, a uniform external appearance was ensured.[3]

With rising concern over hygiene in overcrowded cities, residents took it upon themselves to further control their neighborhoods. In addition to maintaining high property values, they made sure that their immediate surroundings would remain satisfactory. Homeowners formed associations to administer the rules initially put forth by the developers. At the Rock Park Estate (built in 1837) near Liverpool, for example, no one was allowed to purchase property without consenting to the stringent restrictions outlined in the deed of sale and enforced by an association.[4]

The first North American zoning regulations attempted to limit the spread of commercial and industrial areas into residential neighborhoods. The Consolidated Municipal Act of 1904, for example, gave cities in the Province of Ontario the right to regulate the "location, erection and use of buildings for laundries, butcher shops, stores and manufacturers." Through height limitations and minimum setback requirements within sections of the city, early zoning rules contributed substantially to determining the character of neighborhoods. The most far-reaching controls, and the continent's first comprehensive laws, were drafted in 1916 by the Heights of Buildings Commission of New York City. Reform activists joined members of the commission, most of whom were real estate investors, "to save their city from the detrimental impact of the Manhattan skyscraper."[5]

While reformers sought the preservation of light and fresh air at street level, speculators who owned property wanted to limit the rush-hour chaos created by the large number of office building clerks and laborers who had relocated to the area. Although legitimized by the reformers' arguments, this legislation was far from altruistic. In fact, from the beginning, land-use regulations subordinated the interests of health and safety to those of higher property values and profit-making.

Zoning attracted diverse supporters: real estate developers and bankers who saw in it a means to guard investment and secure loans and credit; public administrators, who recognized it as a cost-saving mechanism in the provision of public services; mayors, who saw it as the key to containing blight and preserving the city's tax base; reformers, planners, and architects who sought loftier, determ- inistic design goals, and homeowners, who desired the simple assur- ance of neighborhood stability.[6] For all these reasons, zoning was regarded as essential in North American communities. In 1916, eight cities in the United States had zoning controls. By 1920, the number had jumped to eighty-two, with a total of nine hundred and four zoning ordinances.[7]

Canadian planners keenly observed events south of the border and pushed to make comprehensive zoning a component of their own urban vocabulary. Though it was common practice of Ameri- can municipalities to enact zoning legislation without the presence of a master plan, Canadian planners emulated their British counter- parts' consistent use of comprehensive planning at a first stage. Consequently, in the majority of provinces land-use bylaws must conform to an overall design.[8] A 1904 Toronto bylaw was an early efforts to separate residential from non-residential areas within cities. The first full set of Canadian zoning bylaws was developed in 1924 for Kitchener, Ontario, by planners Thomas Adams and Horace Seymour.

A control mechanism that was proposed to regulate building appearance was deed restriction, a form of privately administered developmental regulation. It is an agreement in a deed that legally binds the holder to certain requirements or provisions that may restrict use or modification of the land by a future buyer. Such restrictions can regulate broad issues like site coverage, density, and use of all buildings on the site. Deed restrictions can address details such as materials chosen and architectural style. In North America, however, legislators can no longer institute restrictions that are in violation of civil rights laws.

Through these methods of control the character of British and

North American suburbs was defined. A homogenous appearance was indicative of a strong community with high values, stability, and a steady increase of property values. Uniformity became more desirable with the Industrial Revolution. To maintain consistency in the face of the vast range of material and construction possibilities was a task of considerable challenge. Ensuring property values by achieving a harmonious aesthetic through architectural controls became ingrained in the residential sector.

Why, then, despite well-established and stringent zoning regulations, codes, bylaws, and fully-staffed planning offices, have new homes put on what seems to me to be a grotesque appearance? Why do established neighborhoods see dwellings demolished in favor of monster-size creations that fail to respect their surroundings? The answer is rooted in societal transformations that saw changes in the place of homes in our value system. It has to do with the basic reason controls were set in the first place: real estate value and the rise of personal wealth.

The well-to-do have always used dwellings to manifest wealth and social status. Sprawling stately homes and palaces with striking architecture on vast estates were a mark of status and riches. Means often implied power to make aesthetic decisions, regardless of aesthetic ability or the surroundings. There are some famous examples of bizarre choices. In Northern Ireland, around the middle of the eighteenth century, Viscount Bangor and Lady Anne Bligh set to build themselves a mansion, but they could not agree on an appropriate style. The Viscount was a Classicist, but his wife was keen on Gothic. When they could not make up their minds, their architect offered an acceptable solution: the front was to be built in Classical style, while the rear in Gothic.[9]

North Americans have their share of grandiose residences, for example, the Vanderbilt Mansion in Hyde Park, New York and Hearst Castle in San Simeon, California. Toronto's Casa Loma boldly expressed the vision of Sir Henry Pellat, who had made his fortune supplying homes with electricity.

With post-World War II prosperity, home ownership became

easier for the middle class. The home quickly evolved from into a mark of achieving the American Dream, and its equivalent in Canada, and the acquisition of a house became a threshold that needed to be crossed to amass personal capital. Since the 1940s, residences have gradually become commodities, at the expense, for some, of emotional attachment. Homeowners factored the value of their homes into their retirement plans. Homes had to look their best to realize the highest possible return on investment.

Developers, designers, and homeowners interpreted municipal controls with a certain aesthetic abandon. They may have respected building height regulations, but opted for a roof resembling a six-teenth-century Tudor mansion, for example. They chose to clad their facades with masonry respecting the letter of the law, but mixed fake stone, brick, and stucco. The inclusion of front multi-car garages transformed the ensemble, making it look at times as if a small dwelling were affixed to the back of a huge garage. When several such odd-looking dwellings stood on the same street, beg-ging for attention, sense of place was given low priority. Municipal regulations were passive and offered very little opposition to issues of "style".

Another compromising factor was lack of professional involvement. Architects commonly design only 5 percent of all resi-dences in North America, most of which are custom-fitted and hardly work with speculative developers. Most homes are designed by technical draftpersons who have rudimentary artchitectural training.

Television shows, glossy magazine spreads, and newspaper articles devoted to "how to increase the real estate value of your home" have mushroomed in recent years. Homeowners are eager to learn more about augmenting the appeal of their property, often at the expense of the community. The increase in the number of wealthy North Americans and easier access to mortgages contri-buted to the rise in the number of McMansions on North America's streets. The 2006 Merill Lynch World Wealth Report showed a growth of 6.8 per cent in the number of American millionaires and a 7.2 percent increase for Canada between 2004 and 2005. Many of the newly rich invested in lavish homes.[10] This trend came to an abrupt halt with the 2008 mortgage meltdown.

Can homes be unique, yet conform to a communal architectural language and foster a sense of place? There are examples of this. They have evolved without control mechanisms or architectural design. The homes on the Greek island of Santorini, for example, with their different shapes and sizes, were all traditionally painted white, and the doorframes mostly light blue, colors that are still respected. The villages of Reggio Calabria in southern Italy are densely built on mountainsides with local stone with consistent building heights. All have red roof tiles, yet each dwelling has its marked distinction within the ensemble.

The tiny Venetian island of Burano, famed for the lace-making skills of its people, has similar characteristics. As one walks along Burano's narrow canals, crossing bridges into alleys, one is struck by the rows of stucco-clad homes. They are painted saffron, ochre, lime or mint green, deep ocean or light blues, brown and reddish-orange, burgundy, purple, and banana yellow. The color sequences do not have an apparent logic, which makes the place even more attention-grabbing. The only common features are white window sashes and shutters painted dark green. The legend goes that Burano's fishermen painted their dwellings so they could distinguish them from afar. Hordes of visitors are drawn to the island. The dwellings, however, do adhere to a hidden code: they are a consistent height, they all have terracotta roof tiles, and the window and door proportions which Burano builders have respected over the centuries give it a coherent appearance.

What is necessary to foster a unique sense of place? Self-imposed discipline, I believe, exercised over a prolonged period of time, centuries perhaps. Beautiful places are born when property owners, designers, and land developers adhere to consistent, if hidden, aesthetic standards, a shared value system, foresight, and, yes, a dose of humility.

Fourteen

The Soapstones of Iqaluit

~

My familiarity with its cultural and physical make-up was rudimentary when I accepted an invitation to visit the city of Iqaluit, the capital of the Territory of Nunavut in the Canadian Arctic. It was a sunny but cool evening in late August when I stepped out of the Discovery Lodge Hotel for a stroll.

The place felt more like an outpost than a town of six thousand inhabitants. It looked as if someone had situated oddly shaped buildings at random distances from the street. A blue-painted gas bar stood next to a home which almost touched a newly built multi-story government building. A short walk on Mivik Road got me to the intersection of Federal and Queen Elizabeth streets. A pickup truck passed by, raising a ball of dust. I could see black mountains, a tall, white building on a hilltop, and the open sea with two large boats. Iqaluit lies above the sixtieth parallel, and there was not a single tree to soften the urban and natural landscapes. The raw, untamed beauty was highlighted by a late evening sun.

I turned along Queen Elizabeth, the main street. It was deserted at this late-evening hour. Three- and four-story aluminum-clad buildings with apartments and offices above stores marked the hub. Right behind, there were brown-painted homes raised above ground to let winter winds pass under them. A snowmobile, a snow motor-cycle, and a *kmotik* sled were parked next to a house, waiting for the winter to arrive. A boat engine and fishing net lay next to another dwelling, probably belonging to a fisherman whose boat was docked in the sea nearby. Seal skins were stretched on a board leaning against an exterior wall for drying. Looking further, I caught a glimpse of large boulders, which drew my interest.

I walked towards a long and narrow single-story gray and blue building. Outside it, I saw several life-sized soapstone sculptures. Beside a bird that looked like an eagle diving down to snap up a fish from the gushing sea was a polar bear cub with its eyes closed resting on a rock. A short distance away, I saw a life-size figure of an Innu couple. The man had his left arm around the woman's shoulders as if to console her. A caribou on the run was etched on a stone nearby. Next to it was the giant sculpted face of a person smoking a traditional pipe. Much like the dwellings, the sculptures were presented unstaged. They were organically embedded in their place of creation, a modest neighborhood near the sea.

As I gazed at the carved soapstones, I realized that they had not only softened a rugged environment, but they also educated those who saw them about the Inuit culture, art, and people. I wondered to what extent what I saw enhanced my perception of this place, and why many societies have made displaying art in public part of their culture.

Can everyday objects, street furniture, for example, be considered art?

Perhaps the most rudimentary expression of artistic endeavor is folk art. In *The Spirit of Folk Art*, Henry Glassie suggests that "it is the result of a people shaping their destiny through the reformulation of heritage, often in the face of colonial threat."[1] Art is one of the means by which culture and tradition are expressed. The artists bring into dynamic association the ideas of individual creativity and collective order.

What, then, is public art? In *Public Art: Thinking Museum Displays Differently*, Hilde Hein writes that, "If private art suggests an intimate exchange, public art gathers a congregation."[2] The viewing of an artwork by the public, irrespective of age, class, or education, is a point of departure. Unlike a museum display, which often targets a specific audience, public art is there for all to see. People go to view private art intentionally, but they come upon public art by chance. It can include every mode of artistic expression, including, by some accounts, even music. Public art, according to Hein, aims to express, and affect, its culture. "If too extreme, it will be rejected or destroyed; if too banal, it will be ignored."

Citizens often feel a sense of entitlement towards a work of art paid for by their tax dollars. It may provoke strong opinions. It may memorialize an event that affected the life of many, by inscribing it in history.

A good place to begin a quest into the genesis of public art is a society such as the Inuit people, whose ancestors roamed the frozen tundra for centuries. Like other old societies, they produced artefacts for functional purposes and for use in rituals aimed at influencing the gods, facilitating travel to other worlds, healing the sick, and foretelling the future. Polar bears, powerful and revered animals, as well as falcons and seals, were featured in many carved objects.[3] Clothing, knives, and the harpoons with which the Inuit hunted seals all had a touch of artistic inventiveness.

Larger-scale creations were vehicles through which spiritual and social purpose was communicated. According to Hein it was "exhortative, commemorative, triumphal, perhaps expressive of collective grief, anger, celebration or occasionally an aggressively provocative act."[2] The ancient Israelis created the golden calf when they grew impatient in the absence of Moses. The Bamyan Buddhas were built in the sixth century along the Asian silk road during the reign of the Indian emperor Kouchin Kanichka, and demolished by the Taliban in 2001. They were a prime example of public art.

Art was expressed on the exterior walls of temples and by statues which paid homage to gods and spirits. Sitting rulers initiated statues or monuments of and for themselves to exercise power, hoping that successive authorities and future generations would keep them long after they were gone. In fact, the French word *monument*, derives from the Latin *monere*, which means "to warn, to recall, to remember". From antiquity, monuments were indispensible elements of public art.[4]

During the Hellenistic period (fourth to first century B.C.) creators of public sculpture continued a long-standing practice of attempting to achieve perfect sculpture-in-the-round. The piece was to be admired from all angles, so it could be central to a public space, focusing attention and defining it, rather than being a decoration. While Greek statues resembled earlier classical works, poses and lines of focus were often twisted, rather than having figures made for straight-on view. The Greeks also developed mosaic art, of which examples have survived.[5]

Roman public art was influenced by, and often imitative of, Greek works, but it was practical. It tended to be detailed if the work did not have a political purpose. The Romans were the first to use concrete in architecture, a major development that allowed construction of structures like the Flavian Amphitheater. It contained sculptures painted in terracotta tones. Roman artists introduced the bust, an image of a person from the shoulders up, as a form of sculpture, for recording the facial features and demeanor of famous or interesting personages.[6]

The Middle Ages, which spanned the period between the fall of the Roman Empire in the fifth century to the beginning of the Early Modern period in the sixteenth century, has given us a vast artistic legacy. It had several large-scale art movements: Byzantine, Celtic, Romanesque, Gothic, and Islamic, among them. Each produced many monuments, often for public display, and included much religious art. The public could view representative figures and scenes imagined by artists of which they had previously only heard.

The era which followed, however, redefined public art. The Renaissance introduced a sense of exhilaration to art. The church played an immense role in the revival of Classical art. It was in Florence where the new movement first saw the creation of significant artistic works. For several centuries, the building of monuments and works of art depicting religious icons and figures under successive generations of the Medici family made the city "a center of splendor".[7] Public art was exhibited in or near cathedrals, on squares, and on buildings.

When Florence's Uffizi Palace was built in the mid-sixteenth century near the River Arno, great attention was given to its exterior, which features sculptures of prominent Tuscan giants in art, science, and politics, such as Donatello and Machiavelli. Works of art were displayed on the façades of other Florentine edifices, and architectural objects or building components, such as wood-carved entry doors, elaborate ironwork on windows, sculpted masonry corners, rooftop edges and eaves were all masterfully crafted. The work, much of which was conceived and enacted during the rule of the Medici family, displayed in public not only a love and patronage of art, but urbanity. It fostered the idea that a building's exterior could evoke celebration and educate passersby as well as complement each other, the streets, and the city.[7]

Renaissance rulers who commissioned magnificent public art also amassed private collections. The period's end saw the introduction of another concept: the museum. In Paris between 1775 and 1789, Comte d'Angiviller, the director-general of the royal buildings, supervised the acquisition of more than two hundred paintings for the royal collection. The Louvre was selected as the site of a hall devoted to art and other fields of knowledge. Internal partitions were removed, skylights installed, and in 1793 the Musée Français was inaugurated. According to Robert Berger in *Public Access to Art in Paris*, it was regarded as "a symbol of the triumph over despotism and as tangible proof of culture born of liberty."[8] Access to the museum was free. It was open to the public three days a week, and on other days, only to artists for the purpose of copying.

Museums served an important role in the cultural education of the public. Their artistic vocabulary was expanded to include subjects other than religion or public figures whose representations were widespread.

The culture of philanthropy emerged during the Industrial Revolution, adding a new dimension to public art. Wealthy industrialists patronized the arts, replacing the rulers of earlier centuries. They laid the foundation for today's private benefactors. The period also saw the emergence of a new form of design. The discipline of industrial design addressed itself to the forms of functional objects for machine production.

At this time new public art was appearing to mark the commemoration, in Europe and North America, of important colonial and local military victories. In the U.S. after the Civil War, for example, many cities erected monuments to the memory of those who fell in battle. Sculptures of generals on horses or of uniformed soldiers were placed in parks and squares and on walls of public buildings.

In the 1930s, a San Francisco businessman engaged the Mexican painter Diego Rivera to paint murals for an exposition that would "glorify industry and technology, promote tourism and symbolize human betterment."[2] One mural featured a female figure which paid homage to the bounty of earth and the labor that transformed it. It was poorly received by the public, who saw it as an expression of socialist sentiments. Rivera inspired young politically-minded artists who would go on to depict working people.

A boost to the creation of public art was given with the creation in 1935 of the American Works Progress Administration program, which subsidized public works, including art. Commissions were given to artists who were traditionally excluded from such awards, including women and people of color.

New forms of expression have expanded the relationship between artwork and a place. Artists such as Christo and Jeanne-Claude created temporary works that attracted large numbers of viewers for short-term engagements. They wrapped buildings, like Berlin's Reichstag in 1995, or the display of wooden gates with saffron-colored fabric hangings that stretched for miles in New York's Central Park in 2005. Other innovative works have engaged the public in sound-making objects, like the one in front of Canada's Ontario Science Centre. Water spouts have become public art. There is one in downtown Atlanta where jets of water trigger others.

Public art has been involved in the actual creation of places using artistic forms in the twentieth century. It has sometimes involved collaboration between several disciplines. The wealthy Spanish businessman Eusebi Güell had learned about the Garden Cities planning concept in England. He wanted to have a similar design for a community for the wealthy on land he owned on the outskirts of Barcelona. He engaged the architect Antonio Gaudí. However, Gaudí's proposal was unpopular with the intended buyers and only two houses were sold, one to the architect himself. The project's public spaces, however, went on to become a magnet for locals and visitors. A row of two-level stone columns resembling trees, serpentine seats enclosing an open square, and an elaborate entrance structure, all covered with colorful ceramic, combined art, landscape, and architectural design.[9]

The work of Israeli sculptor Dani Karavan turned architecture into public art. In the 1968 Negev Monument near the southern town of Beersheba, the artist covered an area of 1,080 square feet (100 square meters) with concrete components, which included desert acacias, objects which made sound when wind passed through them, elements that cast shadows, and lines drawn by streams of water.

Art and architecture have sometimes been combined. Buildings can be regarded as works of art, although they mean to serve a practical function. Such is architect Erich Mendelson's 1921 Einstein Tower, an astrophysical observatory in Potsdam, Germany. It was commissioned by the Einstein Foundation for research related to the physicist's theory of relativity. There are no plane surfaces in the curved building, which was designed to let light from the tele-scope in an upper cupola travel through a shaft into an underground laboratory.

A building which is sometimes regarded as a large-scale sculpture is Le Corbusier's 1955 Chapelle Nôtre-Dame-du-Haut. The renowned Swiss architect moved away from earlier styles towards a free form, which was expressed by angular concrete walls. Situated on a hill above a village, its silo-like white tower and float-ing, curving brown roof give the structure a sculpture-like quality.

The work of contemporary architect Frank O. Gehry falls, as well, into the category of buildings that lean heavily on art. Most of Gehry's work includes curved surfaces that are combined to create free-flowing shapes, best expressed in the Guggenheim Museum in

Bilbao, Spain, which was inaugurated in 1997. It is a suitable building for the display of art, because both the exterior and interior create the bold impression of a work of art. A similar approach was taken by architect Daniel Libeskind in his designs, notably in the Michael Lee-Chin Crystal addition to the Royal Ontario Museum in Toronto, Canada.

A question remains about the social role of public art in place-making. In a talk about his work, German public artist Bonifatius Stirnberg expressed his conviction that public art has this value.[10] Fostering a sense of delight in the life of the city is a key contribution. Public art can stimulate play, creativity, and imagination among children. It promotes contact, communication, and, at times, debate and other forms of dialogue among all members of the community. It accommodates people by incorporating steps, ledges, and benches on which people can sit or lean to appreciate, admire, and reflect. It can bring the various factions of society together by stimulating curiosity and interest in the community's heritage.

The Arctic sun cast long shadows projecting the images of Iqaluit's soapstone sculptures onto the brown soil. There were no museum doors, no guard on duty, just plain-looking houses behind, black mountains in the far distance and sky above. I was fortunate to happen upon this site where I could see, learn, and feel a place, its culture, its people, and its beauty.

Fifteen

Tall Thinking in Amsterdam

THE WATER GLITTERED IN THE CANALS that cross Amsterdam on the bright wintry day when I visited. The row of rusty, habitable barges that docked along the banks moved gently in the water, while their residents carried on with daily chores, from time to time stepping out of the cabins to check on things. A child on his way to school left a house in a row that stood parallel to the waterway. He waved good-bye to his mother, who watched from an upper-floor apartment.

Each of the five- and six-story structures in the row had several tall narrow windows. Brick façades extended above ground-floor stores to roofs decorated with exquisitely sculpted stonework and a date marking their year of construction. A steel rail was affixed to the top of each building; down the road, I saw one being used to hoist a crate so it could be moved in through an upper-story window.

I crossed a curved bridge and walked along the other bank. I got directions from a passerby for how to get to Singel Street. A short while later, I stood in front of number 7, the object of my quest. Squeezed between two larger buildings, it looked timid. It had an articulated crown that could not hide its tiny 3.3-foot (one-meter) width. This was the back of the house, I learned; the front was slightly wider. I took a good look at what locals claim to be the narrowest multistory habitable structure in the world. I continued my walk to Oude Hoogstraat Street and passed in front of number 22, a 6.63-foot (2.02-meter) wide structure. From there, I continued to 26 Kloveniersburgul Street to see one that measured 8 feet (2.44 meters).

The buildings were erected in the sixteenth and seventeenth centuries and seem to have aged well. Windows had obviously been replaced in some cases, elevators installed in others, and stone and brick repaired. I felt as if I were standing in the heart of a giant narrow-front townhouse neighborhood. I was intrigued to think of how successive generations of inhabitants had adapted to living in such quarters. The average width of the houses was about 20 feet (6 meters), equivalent to that of a North American two-car garage. Their length, about 40 feet (12 meters), was not much more than a typical bungalow. Each floor was occupied by a different household, which meant that the occupants of every dwelling lived in an area of 800-1,000 square feet (75-93 square meters). How do they live in such cramped rooms? What luxuries, besides space, do they have to forego? What circumstances make a housing type thrive in one place and be rejected in another? Do such buildings stand a chance to be adopted *en masse* in North America as a way to halt excessive resource consumption and urban sprawl?

Narrow-front homes were born out of regulations in land ownership, and are related to the organization of roads.

The Greek Milesian grid, with streets perpendicular to each other, was introduced by the Romans to the rest of Europe, including England. Its simplicity made it flexible, so, while it did not inherently consider a specific landscape, it was easily adaptable over large areas. The geometric nature of the system ensured an equitable distribution of land. It was easy to attach a price to various lot sizes. Plots became narrow to maximize rental income. They were divided into whatever size and degree of uniformity was necessary. Lots were taxed by frontage size, so it was in the best interest of the landlord to restrict the frontal width to between 13 and 25 feet (4-8 meters). Area could be gained by increased depth, so the tendency was for lots to be long and narrow. The most extreme cases were found on commercial streets, like those next to markets. Encroachment onto the street was common. There were benefits to corner sites because of their two front elevations.[1]

Roman influence lasted in the designation of separate rooms

to specific daily activities, which determined the dwelling's spatial organization.

An interesting innovation in the Middle Ages was the under-croft, a room underneath a building, perhaps the precursor of today's basement, which was used as storage. Its geographic origins are not clear. It seems to have roots within Britain, France, and along the Baltic Sea. By the year 1,100 undercrofts were built on ground level. Despite the high cost, stone remained the primary construction material of these structures. They could withstand the threat of flooding, and provided a firm base for the structure above. Entrances to undercrofts were decorated to become a mark of social status. Undercrofts were commonly used by merchants as adjuncts to their houses.

Shops and covered galleries were common in medieval towns on streets extended from the gates of castles or monasteries. An example is well preserved in the Rows in Chester, England, where the bedrock close to the ground's surface prevented builders from excavating deep cellars. Instead, undercrofts were built just below street level. They were connected to the stalls above with a flight of stairs. These narrow-front rows permitted the co-existence of commercial and residential uses.[2]

The Black Death that struck Europe in the fourteenth century and eliminated at least a third of the population had strong repercussions on traditional institutions. Relief from overcrowding in cities was short-lived. Within a century and half, the population reached pre-epidemic size and continued to grow, creating pressure to expand city boundaries. Relocating fortification walls was out of question, since that would bankrupt the town. The solution was to force densification with taller, narrower buildings.

Dense towns did not necessary imply chaos and overcrowding as shifts in governance made for greater order. Densification was guided by a set of planning principles that included formerly entangled streets being widened and straightened to enhance long vistas. Oversized proportions replaced human scale associated with medieval towns.[3]

Reconfiguration of towns was paralleled by a trend among the nobility to build townhouses. They were designed to have the look and atmosphere of palaces. The number of domestic servants affected the layout and organization of the floor plan.

Narrow-front homes evolved to be domestic dwellings, detached from mixed-use connotations. Once they became fashionable, they were considered a refined generic building type for the masses.

In a typical sixteenth-century Dutch townhouse, two bay windows and an entry door composed the front façade. The ground floor was connected to the street by a couple of steps. Inside the front door was a vestibule. The parlor was in the front, the first room one would enter. Behind the parlor, the dining room, directly above the kitchen, had a view of the back yard. The second-floor, high-ceilinged *piano nobile* ("noble floor") might contain two parlors, one in the front for men, and one at the back for women. The third floor had master and children's bedrooms and the attic was occupied by servants.[3]

While the interior layout of narrow-front homes was standardized, the exterior was more variable, and designed to impress the public. This was evident along Amsterdam's four major canals when I visited, where there are over two thousand such houses. Because of the flow of pedestrians, these buildings were in high demand use as offices and stores as well as homes. The ground floor had a small set of steps, called the *stoop*, which would later be adopted in New York, which was once called New Amsterdam because it was originally settled by the Dutch. The stoops were sometimes abandoned by the developers, who could not otherwise fit in the high ceilings required of *piano nobiles*, and stairs were given added width to create a more luxurious appearance indoors. Outside, spacious gardens were incorporated behind houses that were limited to a maximum length of 100 feet (30 meters). Interior courtyards were sometimes introduced to allow natural light into the dwelling's core.[2]

In England, the typical Georgian-era (1714-1837) narrow-front terrace house consisted of four to six stories. All activities were accommodated on distinct floors. If it could be afforded, an extra floor added luxury and comfort. Naturally, the homes were assessed according to their respective number of stories, as well as their width. The 1666 Great Fire of London led to a series of building acts which aimed to bring uniformity into the shape and construction methods of row houses. In the Great London Building Act of 1774, row houses were classified into four different rates primarily by width and height. The first category consisted of four-story houses over a sunken basement, and the fourth was three stories high above a completely underground basement. Residents occupied different grades, depending on their social class. The wealthy nobility lived in first-grade houses, merchants and professionals in second- and third-grade, and artisans occupied fourth-grade townhouses. It was common for poor families to share a townhouse apartment.[4]

By the eighteenth century, the Palladian style dominated housing design in England's design, in contrast to the Rococo influence in Europe. In parts of North America that were under England's colonial rule, the earliest builders adopted the classical English narrow-front homes as their main pattern of domestic architecture. One of the most notable changes to the design of the townhouse in North America, however, was that it became associated with the moderate- and low-income population. Substandard construction crossed the Atlantic, and the emerging cities of America were just as vulnerable to chaos and poor building practices.

The colonial-era narrow-front homes in Boston's North End, for example, were a mixture; some were inspired by local design and others followed imported ideas. The Revere House, erected about 1680, has urban characteristics as well as elements of the provincial vocabulary in its decorations. These stylistic choices recognized conventions in decoration of street façades with articulated trims and fireplace walls. Debate was more centered on architectural alternatives for the floor plan. Builders wanted to generate a diverse selection of interior arrangements, while keeping a standardized external appearance, to best accommodate the middle class. Most of these dwelling options were simply borrowed from known English patterns.

In cities like Philadelphia, the central staircase plan that allowed for a shop on the front half of the ground floor dominated the streetscape. Sometimes, instead of having an internal corridor to the staircase, there were external passages that branched off from the streets. The central staircase plan divided the house into two vertical segments. Such a building could be configured as front and back tenements, if needed. Many Philadelphia townhouses also had attached back buildings that housed servants and workrooms. This created a space that contained the main and sometimes only staircase of the dwelling.[5]

The evolution of residential development in New York City followed a different pattern. After the Revolutionary War in 1783, with the British gone, the population was half of what it had been eight years earlier. It quickly recovered, tripling within ten years. It became a magnet for people, and a prosperous one as a result of trade with the Caribbean, Europe, and the Orient. Fuelled by immigration, a building boom began.[6] During these years, the Federal style was adopted for the city's narrow-front homes. It remained in vogue until the 1830s. As New York had, in essence, no regional style, it was a transitory departure from the Georgian style into the various classical Revival styles of the 1830s, 1840s, and 1850s. These revivals were not an attempt to copy the ancient styles, but the result of a search for design principles applicable to all forms of architecture.

The evolution of narrow-front homes was affected by various cultural influences. For example, New York incorporated the stoop, the small flight of stairs that led to the first floor front entry, above a high basement. Without any need to protect from flooding, in New York the stoop served a more decorative purpose than a functional one. It began to be seen as a nuisance cluttering the street. However, it permitted a separate front entrance to the kitchen below and gave homeowners a place to lounge casually in front, adding a friendly touch to the neighborhood.

Considerable attention was given to the entryway because it was considered an investment in public display, and front façades were commonly embellished with articulated lintels over doors and windows. Modest narrow-front homes had two stories above a high basement, with a pitched roof and two dormers. By the 1820s the row house was typically wider, and no deeper than two rooms for the sake of adequate sunlight. It had better human scale. This new spatial ratio implied that the rear room on the first floor, too small for the dining room, had to be relocated in the front of the basement, adjacent to the kitchen. This arrangement was especially favorable with servants, as it simplified the frequent walks between the kitchen and the dining room. The time spent eating two to three meals a day in the basement was also more informal than before. Low ceilings, 6½-7 feet (around 2 meters) high, were common for a basement, which must have made the kitchen hot during the summer. With time, as people grew taller, the basement was given more height by excavating deeper, rather than adding steps to the first floor. As there were no cellars indoors, the food was stored underneath the cool ground-level garden. In later decades, the garden was leveled to the floor of the basement. The kitchen, bedrooms, dormers, and the family dining room were all more sparsely decorated than the front facade and the first floor parlors.[6]

Narrow-front homes lent themselves to mass-production, especially when a city had strong demand for housing. Builders specialized in constructing three to four houses for sale at a time. Not surprisingly, they were rarely custom-designed. A small crew of workmen was adequate because of the simplicity of row house construction prior to the introduction of heating and electricity.

From the late seventeenth to the early nineteenth century narrow-front American homes remained stylistically attached to their English and Dutch roots. Nevertheless, there was dynamism in architectural design that continued into the next era; eclecticism brought about change.

When gas lighting was introduced early in the nineteenth century, ceilings, including that of the once-stuffy kitchen, were raised by some 2 feet (0.6 meters).

In the 1830s, industrialized production began to influence building construction, and by the 1840s, machines were used to manufacture doors, moldings, and iron fences, among other components. Indoor flush toilets, hot and cold running water, and heating systems were all considerable innovations that added comfort to everyday life.[7]

After years of copying English architectural handbooks, nineteenth-century America began questioning the relevance of these traditions to the cultural development of the young country. The decline of the Federal style was followed by the introduction of the Greek Revival style during the next several decades. Like the several revival styles that would follow, the results tended to make churches, banks, and residences almost indistinguishable. There was a self-conscious intention to stimulate the emotions by evoking an association with a distant time and place. This was borne of the Romantic idea that "forms were beautiful for the emotions they evoked."[7] But the idea was more the result of an obsession with historic Greek culture. News of the internationally publicized excavations of ancient Greece and Rome reached and captured the interest of many. For example, Greece, the birthplace of democracy, resonated among Americans, who were intent upon eliminating all traces of their colonial past. It is perhaps not so much of a surprise that there is little distinction between the Federal and Greek Revival styles in appearance. Generally, houses fashioned in Greek Revival were distinguished by the recognizable columns and iron work. In addition, the proportions were taller. Instead of the two floors and an attic, there was a complete third floor, and the roof was made shallow and barely visible from the street.

During this era, however, the most significant change was the declining engagement of small-scale builders and attention to craftsmanship. The streetscape seems to have grown more and more homogenous as narrow-front homes were mass-produced. This stirred nostalgia for rural life, and many began to reassess life in the city, laying the foundation for what would later be suburbia.

With plummeting demand for narrow-front homes, cities like Baltimore saw their last construction of luxurious row houses in 1910. Disguised under the name "group homes", they were built for wealthy buyers who did not want the responsibility of maintaining a large garden, but who wanted more than an apartment in the city. Not only did these group homes provide variety, they also served as a buffer between the expensive inner lots and the surrounding less expensive homes.

Providing sufficient daylight was always a major concern for row houses. Daylight rows were used in Baltimore as part of a marketing scheme that incorporated suburban ideals into the row housing design. A seven-room house might measure 20 feet wide and 36 feet deep (6 by 11 meters); the shallowness allowed natural light and fresh air to reach all areas. They were placed on the city's edge, at the end of streetcar lines. Private automobiles were parked at the rear of the rows, often in a built garage.[8]

In the first half of the twentieth century only a handful of known architects included narrow-front houses in their schemes. An influential architect who used them was Bruno Taut, a key figure in Berlin's housing developments. In one suburban project, he planned a neighborhood of ten thousand dwellings. The project was a model development sensitive to the provision of community facilities and included *Reinehause,* or row houses. He argued that properly designed row house units were more conducive to community than large apartment blocks.[2]

After World War II, planners brought forth designs that attempted to combine urban density and some of the characteristics of rural life by creating a model subdivision, moving away from narrow-front homes. The very term was associated with the most squalid conditions of city life.

Just as technological progress had facilitated the mass-production of row houses, further advances did the same for detached houses.

Although there is a resurgence of row housing in some suburbs, the strong drawing power of the single-family detached home makes one wonder, however, whether narrow-front dwellings will ever be popular again in North America, although societal challenges give rise to the prospect that higher density homes, townhouses among them, will no doubt be the focus of attention of planners and architects in years to come.

The need to curb urban sprawl requires reintroduction of dwellings with smaller footprints. Attached townhouses, designed taller, can reduce our spread on the land. Demographic shifts are another reason for rethinking dwelling prototypes. The past few decades have seen growth in types of households that not so long ago were considered marginal. Single people, single-parent families, childless couples, as well as seniors now constitute a large segment of the population. Many are not seeking to live in single-family detached homes, but wish to reside in ground-related units which are not part of an apartment complex. Narrow-front housing, where each household has its apartment, is a solution that also offers access to a backyard. The narrow width, coupled with new technologies, offers the possibility of freeing the dwelling's interior from bearing partitions and flexibility to arrange layouts according to the financial capabilities and lifestyle of the inhabitant.

As I continued my walk along Amsterdam's canals, crossing over from bank to bank in search of narrow homes, I realized that we can look to the past to discover what we ought to build in the future.

Sixteen

The Spirit of Assisi

GAZING AT A MAP, I CONSIDERED ALTERNATE travel routes. It was mid-afternoon and I still needed to find lodging after a long drive on the serpentine roads of Italy's Umbria region. I was close to the town of Assisi. If I hurried, I could still make it to the Basilica of St. Francis and see its architecture and art.

Built on a hill and surrounded by olive groves and cypress trees, Assisi stretches out along the slopes of Mount Sabassio between the Tescio, Topino, and Chiascio rivers. It dates back to Umbrian, Etruscan, and Roman times. It is the birthplace of two notable religious figures who influenced the city's history and the Catholic faith: St. Francis, born in 1182, after whom the Basilica was named, and St. Clare, born in 1193.

I parked outside the walls and began a brisk walk uphill. I passed through Porta Nuova and arrived at a square crowded with shaven-headed Franciscan monks in brown robes, nuns dressed in gray, lay worshipers, and other locals. Carved icons above entrance doors adorned brownstone buildings and religious artefacts were on sale in stores. A serene silence was occasionally punctuated by church bells.

Flocks of white pigeons flew overhead when I reached the long-arched colonnade of Piazza Inferiore at the front of the Basilica. I rushed up a stairway and approached a tall doorway. "Visiting hours are over." A uniformed guard gestured and apologized, seeing my disappointment. I tried arguing, to no avail, saying that I had come from afar. As I walked back down the steps, I noticed a group entering the crypt on the lower level of the church. I followed behind and passed through a double-vaulted portal to a T-shaped space. It led to an interior with two transepts and a semi-circular apse.

Episodes from the life of St. Francis depicted on the blue-painted ceiling vaults were illuminated by artificial light. I sat down on a wooden bench, staring at the images and the space. Suddenly, the crisp voice of a woman singing in Spanish accompanied by a guitar sounded out. After she sang several verses, a group sang along to the chorus. The melody was beautiful and the singers were clearly in the moment. It felt as if they were trying to draw the attention of an invisible spirit. The singing lasted a few minutes, but it touched the soul and tugged on sensitive heart strings. When the group left, I remained seated, wondering why what I just heard was so moving. I did not understand the lyrics, nor did I know the melody or the people, yet it spoke to me. Was the sacred place the reason for my emotions? Perhaps. It is a site of pilgrimage for many people.

Of the places we have visited, there are those which live in us long after the voyage has ended. Something in them inexplicably affects us, spiritually. Our mental state at the moment may have caused it, yet something in the location, be it a mountaintop or a church, served as a backdrop, a trigger perhaps, for its occurrence. Called "sacred", such spots have a unique sense of place worth deciphering.

In *Landscapes of the Sacred*, Belden Lane introduces several axioms to categorize and define such places.[1] Sacred spots are not chosen; they do the choosing. Despite our best efforts and desires to find them and experience their hidden forces they find us. We may happen to stumble upon them, much like what occurred to me in Assisi. "Sacred place is ordinary ritually made extraordinary," he writes. Some places look simple and unassuming to the naked eye, yet their past association with historical, mythical, or spiritual events has endowed them with hidden powers. In *The Substance of Things Seen: Art, Faith, and the Christian Community*, Robin Jensen defines a sacred space as "a site where we have a means to rise and descend through an open door to the unknown and the eternal."[2]

The quest for communication with divine powers has been part of human existence since ancient times. Mountaintops and forest clearings have been sites where bands practiced spiritual rites. The artefacts used to draw the attention of gods were simple: fire, masks, or figurines, next to which prayers were chanted and sacrifices made. When nomadic tribes settled down, they erected permanent places, temples, and statues. Each faith or civilization was guided by traditions, yet several common threads can be found in many of these sites.

Spiritual places have a clear demarcation. They may be remote, markedly distinguished from their surroundings or set at a distance from other edifices. To reach the Monastery of St. Catherine in the Sinai Peninsula, for example, one needs to venture deep into a desert and climb a mountain.

Crossing a threshold is another aspect. Traversing a line, a built artefact, or a distinctive space, one leaves behind the secular world to enter the divine. Sacred spaces may be entered via a bridge, a tunnel, an enormous archway, or an oversized plaza. Often a gesture such as removing one's shoes, kneeling, reciting prayers, or touching an object is performed upon entry.

Spiritual places are sites of past special occurrences. I was drawn to Assisi, knowing that it was a center of faith and a site of miracles, expecting to see pilgrims. Jews, for example, flock to touch, pray, or place wish-notes in the cracks of Jerusalem's Western Wall, a remnant of the destroyed Holy Temple, and Muslim pilgrims visit Mecca to fulfill the fifth pillar of Islam, a journey that every faithful Muslim tries to do once in a lifetime. By the accounts of some faiths, sacred places are sites from which forces radiate.

The design of primarily religious buildings was traditionally based on sacred geometry. In *Spiritual Path, Sacred Path: Myth, Ritual and Meaning in Architecture*, Thomas Barrie suggests that their aim was twofold: to create a self-contained and unified whole, and "to reflect God's perfection."[3] The Egyptian Pyramid of Cheops corresponds to Golden Section proportions. India's Taj Mahal in Agra has a system of proportions that is interrelated with the surrounding buildings. Greek temples from the Classical era, such as the Parthenon on the Acropolis, also correspond to the Golden Section. In designing the old Sacristy in San Lorenzo in Florence, Renaissance architect Filippo Brunnelleschi used complex geometry to calculate relationships between the building's various parts.

Sacred places have been, and are, settings where rituals are performed. Each faith has its own, and at times the practices are unique to a particular place of worship and have to be performed by all visitors. The quest for sacred experience has long been one of many travelers' goals.

People risk their lives and spend life savings crossing vast distances for a divine experience. Some three hundred million "faith tourists" spend $18 billion a year on pilgrimages, for example.[4] On their multistop voyages, some follow a route such as *el Camino de Santiago* (The Way of St. James), a pilgrimage to the Cathedral of Santiago de Compostela in Galicia, Spain. Other known pilgrimage destinations are Uman, Ukraine, the grave of the Rabbi Nachman of Breslov, and Mount Kailash in Tibet where thousands of Buddhists and others head each year.

Designers who were entrusted with the design of places of worship labored to come up with architectural ideas which could inspire spiritual experiences. In *Space and Spirit*, Sigurd Bergmann suggests that architecture is a "constellation of symbols, one in which human ideas are brought together and materialized in a building."[5] She argues that buildings and their surroundings have no immediate connection to the human subject or to physical objects. "Atmosphere emerges, however, when these two elements meet." It was this quest to join two seemingly unconnected solitudes that drove architects who created sacred buildings. Imaginative cathedrals, churches, and temples have been built throughout the ages, many of them striving to defy the laws of physics and exceed height or span limits.

A building whose construction began in 1883 and is still ongoing is the Sagrada Familia Cathedral by Antonio Gaudí in Barcelona, Spain. The uncommon design draws worshipers and the curious from near and far, who come to see the sculpture-like structure. Gaudi regarded churches as the most representative buildings of a people. He filled the place with patron saints, biblical figures and selected biblical episodes, and religious texts.[6] The striking interior contains very tall, tree-like stone pillars and carved objects. The space where the nave meets the transept is covered by a large vault, under an imposing tower.

The introduction of modern means of construction at the dawn of the twentieth century was instrumental in helping architects introduce new forms and break with tradition while conceiving of places of worship. Reinforced concrete and steel construction permitted wide, tall open spaces. Frank Lloyd Wright's 1941 Annie Pfeifer Memorial Chapel in Lakeland, Florida, is such a place. The building is composed of jagged, rectangular shapes and a tower over a two-level auditorium made of angular lines. Philip Johnson's 1960 Roofless Church in New Harmony, Indiana is a simple canopy rising from the inside and anchored to concrete plinths. In the Tokyo Cathedral, Japanese architect Kenzo Tange designed a tower whose rounded glass cupola is lying on its side to suggest both strength and shelter. Another celebrated chapel is Le Corbusier's Nôtre-Dame-du-Haut at Ronchamp in France. Inaugurated in 1955, it is set on grass with trees in the background and has a sculpture-like presence. Its unique lighting comes from various-size openings along one wall. Lighting plays an important role in creating a unique sacred sense.

Skillfully designed places of worship can inspire visitors. The question, however, is whether the draw of formal spiritual experiences and religion are as strong now as they were some half-century ago when the above-described places were constructed. A 2002 study published in the American Sociological Review suggests that the percentage of Americans who said they had no religious preference has doubled in less than ten years, rising from 7 to 14 percent of the population. A survey by the Pew Research Center found that 20 percent of 18- to 25-year-olds reported no religious affiliation, up from just 11 percent in the late 1980s.[7]

With diminished attendance at formal places of worship, are they the only locations of spiritual experiences? Can we be moved anywhere, in an unexpected or unchoreographed setting?

Life can hand us special moments, occurrences, a situation perhaps, where we step out of our mundane routine to be part of, see, or feel events that touch us in an inexplicable fashion, where we get to experience an unknown side of ourselves or others, where the world moves us in a special way.

Special moments, much like spiritual experiences, find us. We might ease their coming by making room for them in our minds. But for some, these rooms are cluttered with other matters. The daily routine leaves fewer hours for personal reflection and quality time with loved ones. Constant exposure to media stories and images of hunger, war, and despair makes us lose hope. Spirituality has a communal dimension, and it seems that our capacity to draw comfort from fellow beings is being reduced.

Long line-ups of single-occupant cars in the morning and afternoon rush hours mean that fewer people are sharing seats in public transit. Opportunities for an exchange between strangers or innocent talk between schoolchildren on their way to school have diminished. Today it looks as if the entire world is plugged into a playback device of some kind. At the office, we tend to spend more time gazing at computers and less in face-to-face conversations with colleagues.

There are also automatic teller machines in banks, self-serve gas stations, unmanned checkout counters in grocery stores, ticket machines in theaters, automated answering messages in company phone directories, mechanized checkout of books in libraries, and plenty of vending machines to replace cafeterias. They switch off human contact, a breeding ground for special moments. And what about the effect of a place on special moments? Many sacred sites and sites of repose have disappeared.

Contemporary dwelling design and lifestyle seem to minimize personal interaction. Each room has its own information appliance and every family member has a TV set. Conversation which crosses ages during dinnertime is often drowned in overbooked after-hours social agendas. Moments that could have sprung up when parents and children collaborate on a school project are slowly fading away.

The outdoors no longer offers much comfort or opportunity for exchange either. The number of meeting places and their quality has diminished. Neighborhoods, built for seclusion, have fewer people, fewer or no sidewalks, walking or bike paths, benches, or civic squares. We have fewer public markets or corner stores.

Good places which foster special moments and lead to unique experiences can be recreated. The fundamentals need not be forgotten and they can be redesigned into new and existing communities. After all, they make us who we are.

Sources

Chapter One. Teatime in Istanbul

[1]Erlande-Brandenburg, A. *The Cathedral: the Social and Architectural Dynamics of Construction.* Cambridge: Cambridge University Press, 1989.

[2]Carnage, D. H. S. *Cathedrals and How They Were Built.* Cambridge: Cambridge University Press, 1948.

[3]Allen, E. *Fundamentals of Building Construction Material and Methods.* New York: John Wiley & Sons, 1990.

[4]Collins, P. *Changing Ideals in Modern Architecture.* Montreal: McGill University Press, 1965.

[5]Tafuri, Manfredo and Francesco Dal Co. *Modern Architecture.* New York: Electra/Rizzoli, 1986.

Chapter Two. Fiore Di Zucchini in Montepulciano

[1]Peyton, J. *Pub Scene.* West Sussex: Wiley-Academy, 2006.

[2]Ryder, B. *Restaurant Design.* London: Laurence King Publishing Ltd., 2004.

[3]Franck, K. A. *Food + Architecture.* London: Wiley-Academy, 2002.

[4]Kiefer, N. M. "Economics and the Origin of the Restaurant," *Cornell Hotel and Restaurant Administration Quarterly,* August 2002.

[5]Jacobs, M. and P. Scholliers. *Eating Out in Europe: Picnics, Gourmet Dining, and Snacks Since the Late Eighteenth Century.* Oxford: Berg Publishers, 2003.

[6]*McDonald's Corporation.* <http://www.mcdonalds.com/corp/about/mcd_history_pg1.html> Accessed February 8, 2008.

[7]Biing-Hwan J., J. Guthrie, and E. Frazao, "Away-from-Home Foods Increasingly Important to Quality of American Diet," U.S. Department of Agriculture, Economic Research Service, Agriculture Information Bulletin no. 749, 1999.

[8]National Restaurant Association, <www.restaurant.org> Accessed May 1, 2008.

[9]Kaplan, M. *Theme Restaurants.* New York: Rizzoli International Publications, 1997.

[10]Lohmeyer, L. "Ambiance, Design Key to Attracting Consumers' Palates," *Nation's Restaurant News,* October 4, 2004.

[11]"Walkthrough: into the Blue". *Interior Design,* July, 2007.

[12]Oldenburg, R. *The Great Good Place: Cafés, Coffee Shops, Bookstores, Bars, Hair Salons, and Other Hangouts at the Heart of a Community,* New York: Marlowe & Company, 1989.

Further reading:
Ellis, M. *The Coffee House: A Cultural History.* London: Weidenfeld & Nicolson, 2004.

"Americans Are Dining out in Record Numbers and It Shows," *Food and Drink Weekly,* May 29, 2000. http://findarticles.com/p/articles/mi_m0EUY/is_21_6/ai_62827843, Accessed February 8, 2008.

Spang, R. L. *The Invention of the Restaurant.* Cambridge: Harvard University Press, 2000.

Chapter Three. Crowding in Hong Kong

[1]Government of Hong Kong. "GovHK: Living in Hong Kong," <http://www.gov.hk/en/nonresidents/>, Accessed April 29, 2008.

[2]Lynch, K. *City Sense and City Design.* Cambridge: MIT Press, 1990.

[3]Jackson, F. *Sir Raymond Unwin: Architect, Planner and Visionary.* London: Zwemmer, 1985.

[4]MacBurnie, I. *Reconsidering the Dream: Towards a Morphology for Mixed Density Block Structure in Suburbia.* Vol. 1. Ottawa: Canada Mortgage and Housing Corporation, 1992.

[5]Stilgoe, J. R. *Borderland: Origins of the American Suburb, 1820-1838.* New Haven: Yale University Press, 1988.

[6]Marsh, M. *Suburban Lives*. New Brunswick: Rutgers University Press, 1990.

[7]Wright, G. *Building the American Dream*. Cambridge: MIT Press, 1981.

[8]Muller, P. O. *Contemporary Suburban America*. Englewood Cliffs, NJ: Prentice Hall, 1981.

[9]Goldberg, M., and J. Mercer. *The Myth of the North American City: Continentalism Challenged*. Vancouver: University of British Columbia Press, 1986.

[10]Institute of Traffic Engineers. *Recommended Practice for Subdivision Streets*. Washington: 1965.

[11]Southwarth, M., and E. Ben-Joseph. *Streets and the Shaping of Towns and Cities*. New York: McGraw-Hill, 1997.

[12]Schwela, D. and O. Zali. *Urban Traffic Pollution*. London: E. & F.N. Spon, 1999.

[13]Low, N., B. Gleeson, R. Green and D. Radovic. *The Green City: Sustainable Homes, Sustainable Suburbs*. Sydney, Australia: University of New South Wales Press, 2005.

[14]Organization for Economic Co-Operation and Development. *Motor Vehicle Pollution—Reduction Strategies Beyond 2010*. Paris, 1995.

[15]Natural Resources Canada. *Energy Efficiency Trends in Canada, 1990 to 2003*. June 2005: 17.

[16]Kunstler, J. H. *The Geography of Nowhere: the Rise and Decline of America's Man-Made Landscape*. New York: Touchstone Books, 1994.

[17]Morrison, M. L. *Historic Savannah: Survey of Significant Buildings in the Historic and Victorian Districts of Savannah, Georgia*. Savannah: Historic Savannah Foundation, 1979.

Chapter Four. Turnips in Dalian
[1]Schoenauer, N. *6000 Years of Housing*. New York: Garland STPM Press, 1981.

[2]Harper, D. *Dictionary.com*. http://dictionary.reference.com/browse/market, Accessed Jan 19, 2008.

[3]Calibi, D. *The Market and the City: Square, Street and Architecture in Early Modern Europe.* Hampshire: Ashgate Publishing Ltd., 2004.

[4]Varchi, B. *Storie fiorentine*, notes ed. G. Milanseni (Florence, 1857-58), vol. IX, ch. XXIX.

[5]Wolfe, M. W. "The Bazaar at Istanbul." *The Journal of the Society of Architectural Historians*, Vol. 22, No. 1. (Mar., 1963), pp. 24-28.

[6]Lennard, S. H. C. and H. L. Lennard. *Public Life in Urban Places.* Southampton, N.Y.: Gondolier Press, 1984.

[7]Tangires, H. *Public Markets and Civic Culture in Nineteenth-Century America.* Baltimore: The Johns Hopkins University Press, 2003.

[8]Humphrey, K. *Shelf Life: Supermarkets and the Changing Cultures of Consumption.* Cambridge, UK: Cambridge University Press, 1998.

[9]Adler, J. "Take Out Nation," *Newsweek*, February 9, 2004.

[10]Brown, A. "Counting Farmer's Markets," *The Geographical Review.* 91 (4), October 2001, pp. 655-674.

[11]Brown, A. "Farmers' Market Research 1940-2000: An Inventory and Review," *American Journal of Alternative Agriculture*, Vol. 17, No. 4, 2002.

[12]Summer, R. and M. Wing. "Farmers' Markets Please Their Customers," *California Agriculture*, April 1980, p. 10.

[13]Curry, J. and H. Oland. *Prince George and Region Public Market Study.* Prince George, B.C.: University of Northern British Columbia Environmental Studies Program, 1998.

[14]Schneider, E. "How a New Farmers' Market Can Make an Old City Bloom," *The New York Times*, Wednesday, June 20, 1990.

[15]Humphrey, K. *Shelf Life: Supermarkets and the Changing Cultures of Consumption.* Cambridge, UK: Cambridge University Press, 1998.

Further reading:

Hightower, J. *Eat Your Heart Out.* New York: Crown Publishers, Inc., 1975.

Chapter Five. Hugging in Casole D'Elsa

[1]Margulis, H. L. "Homebuyer choices and search behavior in a distressed urban setting," *Housing Studies*, 3:2, 112-133, 1988.

[2]Statistics Canada. *Average Hours Per Week of Television Viewing.* <www.statcan.ca/English/Pgdb/arts23.htm>. Catalogue no. 87F0006XPE, 2003.

[3]Friedman, A., *Sustainable Residential Development: Planning and Design Principles of Homes and Communities.* New York: McGraw Hill, 2007.

[4]Busch, A. *Geography of Home.* New York: Princeton Architectural Press, 1999.

[5]Bryant, W. K. and C. D. Zick. "An Examination of Parent-Child Shared Time," *Journal of Marriage and the Family.* 58 (Febru-ary, 1996): 227-237.

Chapter Six. Swings in Petach Tikva

[1]Eriksen, A. *Playground Design.* New York: Van Nostrand Reinhold Company, Inc., 1985.

[2]Mumford, L. *The City in History: Its Origins, Its Transformations and Its Prospects.* New York: Harcourt, Brace and World, 1961.

[3]Plumb, J. H. *Studies In Social History.* London: Longmans Green, 1955.

[4]Solomon, S. *American Playgrounds: Revitalizing Community Space.* Lebanon, NH: University Press of New England, 2005.

[5]Tai, L., M. T. Haque, G. K. McLellan and E. J. Knight. *Designing Outdoor Environments for Children: Landscaping Schoolyards, Gardens and Playgrounds.* New York: McGraw-Hill, 2006.

[6]Aggarwal, M. *Outdoor Play Areas for Children in High-Density Housing in Montreal.* Thesis submitted to Minimum Cost Housing Program in McGill University, 2001.

[7]Cavallo, D. *Muscles and Morals.* Haney Foundation, 1981.

[8]Sealander, J. *The Failed Century of the Child: Governing America's Young in the Twentieth Century.* Cambridge, UK: Cambridge University Press, 2003.

[9]Swanson, R. A. and B. Spears. *History of Sport and Physical Education in the United States.* Boston: McGraw-Hill, 1995.

[10]Lefaivre, L. and I. de Roode, *Aldo Van Eyck: The Playgrounds and the City.* Amsterdam: NAi Publishers Rotterdam, 2002.

[11]Eriksen, A. *Playground Design.* New York: Van Nostrand Reinhold Company, Inc., 1985.

[12]Postman, N. *The Disappearance of Childhood.* New York: Delacorte Press, 1982.

[13]Larson, R. W. "How U.S. Children and Adolescents Spend Time: What It Does (and Doesn't) Tell Us About Their Development," *Current Directions in Psychological Science,* Vol. 10, No. 5, October 2001.

[14]Flammer, A. and B. Schaffner. "Adolescent Leisure Across European Nations," *New Directions for Child and Adolescent Development,* No. 99, Spring 2003.

[15]Dubas, J. S. "Longitudinal changes in the time parents spend in activities with their adolescent children as a function of child age, pubertal status, and gender," *Journal of Family Psychology,* Vol. 16, No. 4, 2002: 415-427.

[16]Bryant, W. K. and C. D. Zick. "An Examination of Parent-Child Shared Time," *Journal of Marriage and the Family.* 58, Feb. 1996: 227-237.

[17]Environmental research foundation, and P. Montague, ed. "TV Viewed as a Public Health Threat," *Rachel's Environment and Health Weekly* 681, Jan. 6, 2000. <http://www. sustainingwisconsin .org/issue.papers/pdf/bp-tune-2.pdf>

[18]Gallo, A. E. "Food Advertising in the United States," in *America's Eating habits: Changes and Consequences,* edited by Elizabeth Frazao, Agriculture Information Bulletin no. 750. Washington: U.S. Department of Agriculture, 1999.

[19]Orr, D. W. "Political Economy and the Ecology of Childhood." In *Children and Nature: Psychological, Sociocultural and Evolutionary Investigations,* P. H. Kahn, Jr. and S. R. Kellert, eds. Cambridge, MA: Massachusetts Institute of Technology, 2002: 279-304.

[20]Tremblay, M. S., Williams, J. D. "Is the Canadian childhood

obesity epidemic related to physical inactivity?" *International Journal of Obesity and Related Metabolic Disorders*, 27, 1100-1105, 2003.

[21]Carrière, G. "Parent and child factors associated with youth obesity," *Health Reports—Supplement*, 14, 29-39. Catalogue no. 82-003-XIE, 2003.

[22]Louv, R. *Last Child in the Woods: Saving Our Children from Nature-Deficit Disorder*. Chapel Hill, NC: Algonquin Books of Chapel Hill, 2005.

Chapter Seven. Wandering in Tijuana

[1]Natural Resources Canada. *Energy Efficiency Trends in Canada, 1990 to 2003*. June 2005. 17.

[2]AWWA Research Foundation and American Water Works Association. *Residential End Uses of Water*. Prepared by Mayer, P. W. and W. DeOreo et al., U.S.A., 1999.

[3]Office of Energy Efficiency. *The State of Energy Efficiency in Canada, Report 2006*. Ottawa, ON: Energy Publications, Office of Energy Efficiency, 2006.

[4]U.S. Energy Information Administration. *Table 2.2 Residential Sector Energy Consumption*. Official Energy Statistics from the U.S. Government. http://www.eia.doe.gov/emeu/mer/consump.html, Accessed 2006.

[5]Natural Resources Canada. *Energy Efficiency Trends in Canada, 1990 to 2003*. June 2005. 17.

[6]Nebraska Energy Office. http://www.neo.state.ne.us/home_const/factsheets/min_use_lumber.htm, Accessed 2006.

[7]Canada Mortgage and Housing Corporation (CMHC). *Practice for Sustainable Communities*. Ottawa, 2000.

[8]Canada Mortgage and Housing Corporation (CMHC). *Practice for Sustainable Communities*. Ottawa, 2000.

[9]Brundtland Commission, *Our Common Future*, Oxford, New York: Oxford University Press, 1987.

[10]Bullock, N. and M. Takoff. *Greening the Grow Home: The Use of Recycled Products in Building Materials*. Undergraduate Project Report, Department of Civil Engineering and Applied Mechanics. Montreal: McGill University, 1993.

Chapter 8. E-mails from Broughton Hall

[1]Pelegrin-Genel, E. *Büro, Schönheit, Prestige, Phantasie.* Cologne: DuMont, 1996.

[2]Badawy, A. *A History of Egyptian Architecture.* Berkeley/Los Angeles: University of California Press, 1968.

[3]Le Mollé, R. and G. Vasari. *Im Dienst der Medici.* Stuttgart: Klett-Cotta, 1998.

[4]Schumman-Bacia, E. *Die Bank von England und ihr Architekt John Soane.* Zürich / Munich: Verlag für Architektur Artemis, 1989.

[5]Albrecht, D. and C. B. Broikos, eds. *On the Job: Design and the American Office.* New York: Princeton Architectural Press, 2000.

[6]*The Principles of Scientific Management,* published 1911.

[7]Hascher, R., S. Jeska and B. Klauck, eds. *A Design Manual: Office Buildings.* Basel, Germany: Birkhäuser, 2002.

[8]Worthington, J., ed. *Reinventing the Workplace.* Oxford: Architectural Press, 1997.

[9]Friedman, T. L. *The World is Flat: A Brief History of the Twenty-First Century.* New York: Farrar, Straus and Giroux, 2006.

[10]Marmot, A. *Office Space Planning: Designing for Tomorrow's Workspace.* New York: McGraw-Hill, 2000.

[11]Wilson, C. "Home sweet office for IKEA's workers". *The New York Times,* Sunday, February 11, 2007, p. 32.

Further reading:

Basso, P. *Modern Times, Ancient Hours: Working Lives in the Twenty-First Century.* London: Verso, 1998.

Duffy, F., C. Cave and J. Worthington, eds. *Planning Office Space.* London: The Architecture Press Ltd., 1976.

Zelinsky, M. *The Inspired Workspace: Designs for Creativity and Productivity.* Gloucester, MA: Rockport Publishers Inc., 2002.

"Welcome to Broughton Hall" <http://www.broughtonhall.co.uk/main.html>, Accessed March 9, 2007.

Chapter Nine. The Winds of Fargo

[1]Ferguson, W. M. *The Anasazi of Mesa Verde and the Four Corners.* Niwot, Colorado: University of Colorado Press, 1996.

[2]Wines, J. *Green Architecture.* Köln: Taschen, 2000.

[3]Burenhult, G., Ed. "The Megalith Builders of Western Europe." *People of the Stone Age: Hunter-gatherers and Early Farmers.* San Francisco: Harper, 1993.

[4]Ritchie, A. *Prehistoric Orkney.* London: B.T. Batsford, Ltd/ Historic Scotland, 1995.

[5]Rudofsky, B. *Architecture without Architects.* New York: Doubleday & Compancy, Inc., 1965.

[6]Duly, C. *The Houses of Mankind.* London: Thames and Hudson, Ltd, 1979.

Chapter Ten. The Heart of York

[1]Sitte, C. *The Art of Building Cities.* New York, NY: Reinhold Publishing Corporation, 1945.

[2]Moughtin, Cliff. *Urban Design: Street and Square.* Oxford: Butterworth-Heinemann Ltd., 1992.

[3]Zucker, P. *Town and Square: From the Agora to the Village Green.* Cambridge: MIT Press, 1970.

[4]Corbett, N. *Transforming Cities: Revival in the Square.* London: RIBA Enterprises, 2004.

[5]Soderstrom, M. *Green City: People, Nature, and Urban Life.* Montreal: Véhicule Press, 2006.

[6]Zucker, P. *Town and Square.* New York: Columbia University Press, 1959.

[7]Corbett, N. *Transforming Cities: Revival in the Square.* London: RIBA Enterprises, 2004.

[8]Webb, M. *The City Square.* New York: Watson-Guptill Publications, 1990.

[9]Mumford, L. *The City in History: Its Origins, Its Transformations, and its Prospects.* New York: Harcourt, Brace & World, Inc., 1961.

[10]Crowhurst Lennard, S.H. and H. L. Lennard. *The Wisdom of Cities.* Carmel, California: International Making Cities Livable, 2002.

[11]Lawrence, H. W. "The Greening of the Squares of London: Transformation of Urban Landscapes and Ideals," *Annals of the Association of American Geographers*, 83 (1), 1993, pp. 90-118.

[12] ummerson, J. *Architecture in Britain 1530-1830*. Harmondsworth, UK: Penguin Books, 1977.

[13]Youngson, A. J. *The Making of Classical Edinburgh, 1750-1840*. Edinburgh: Edinburgh University Press, 1966.

[14]Longstaffe-Gowan, T. "Gardening and the Middle Classes, 1700-1830", in *London's Pride: The Glorious History of the Capital's Gardens*, ed. Mireille Galinou. London: Anaya Publishers, 1990.

[15]Olmsted, F. L. *The Years of Olmsted, Vaux and Company, 1865-1874*. Vol 6 of *The Papers of Frederick Law Olmsted*. Baltimore: Johns Hopkins University Press, 1992.

[16]Frommer, A. in *The St. Albans Group & Wal-Mart Stores, Inc., Land Use Permit #6F0471*, June 13, 1994, Exhibit C-8, at page 4.

[17]In *re Wal-mart Stores, Inc. 702 A.2d 397* (Vt. 1997).

[18]Friert, M. "Top social networks: Facebook grows while MySpace slows," *Compete.com*, accessed May 14, 2007, at <http://blog.compete.com/2007/05/14/top-social-networks-april-facebook-myspace/>

Further reading:

Bacon, E. *Design of Cities*. New York: Random House, 1965.

Batty, M. "The Size, Scale and Shape of Cities," *Science*, Vol. 319, 8 Feb. 2008, pp. 769-771.

Crowhurst Lennard, S.H. and H. L. Lennard. *Livable Cities*. Southampton, NY: Center for Urban Well-Being, 1987.

Crowhurst Lennard, S.H. and H. L. Lennard. *Making Cities Livable*. Gondolier Press, 1997.

Duany, A. and E. Plater-Zyberk. *Towns and Town-Making Principles*. New York: Rizzoli, 1991.

Lucic, K. *Human Scale in the Urban Design of Montreal Residential Developments*. Graduate Thesis submitted to McGill University School of Architecture, 1995.

Santori, S. A. S. *Lucca and Its Surroundings*. Bologna, Italy: Officina Grafica Bolognese, 2004.

Sitte, C. *City Planning According to Artistic Principles*. Translated from the German by George R. Collins and Christiane Crasemann Collins. New York: Random House, 1965.

Chapter Eleven. The Kitchen of Pina and Felice

[1]Jokilehto, J. *A History of Architectural Conservation*. Oxford: Butterworth Heinemann, 1999.

[2]Ouf, A. "Authenticity and the Sense of Place in Urban Design." *Journal of Urban Design*, 6.1., 2001, pp 73-86.

[3]Hollister, W.C. *Medieval Europe: A Short History*. New York: McGraw-Hill, 1994.

[4]Earl, J. *Building Conservation Philosophy*. Reading, U.K.: The College of Estate Management, 1996.

[5]Boyer, C. "City of Collective Memory: Its Historical Imagery and Architectural Elements." *Urban Design: Reshaping our Cities*, eds. A. V. Moudon and W. Attoe. Seattle: University of Washington, 1995, pp. 82-83.

[6]Jokilehto, J. *A History of Architectural Conservation*. Oxford: Butterworth Heinemann, 1999.

[7]Knox, P.L. and S.A. Marston. *Places and Regions in Global Context: Human Geography*. New Jersey: Prentice Hall, 2001.

[8]Feilden, B. *Conservation of Historic Buildings*. Boston: Butterworth Scientific, 1982.

[9]Kain, R. "Introduction: Definitions, Attitudes and Debates." *Planning for Conservation*, ed. R. Kain. London: Mansell, 1981, pp. 1-16.

[10]Moudon, A.V. *Built for Change: Neighborhood Architecture in San Francisco*. Cambridge: MIT Press, 1986.

[11]Slater, T.R. "The Birmingham Jewellery Quarter: Cultural Continuity in Practice." *Urban Design: Reshaping our Cities*, eds. A.V. Moudon and W. Attoe. Seattle: University of Washington, 1995, pp. 67-75.

Chapter Twelve. Pathways in Kfar Sava

[1]Canadian Institute for Health Information. *Improving the Health of Canadians*. Ottawa, 2004.

[2] Schoenauer, N. *6000 Years of Housing*. New York: W. W. Norton, 2000.

[3] Howard, E. *Garden Cities of Tomorrow* (original 1898 title: *Tomorrow: A Peaceful Path to Real Reform*). London: Swan Sonnenschein, 1902.

[4]Macfadyen, D. *Sir Ebenezer Howard and the Town Planning Movement*. Manchester: Manchester University, 1933.

[5]Parsons, K.C. "British and American Community Design: Clarence Stein's Manhattan Transfer, 1924-74." *Planning Perspectives* 7:191-210, 1992.

[6]Gans, H. J. *The Levittowners*. New York: Pantheon Books, 1967.

[7]Van der Ryn, S. and P. Calthorpe. *Sustainable Communities: A New Design Synthesis for Cities, Suburbs and Towns*. San Francisco: Sierra Club Books, 1986.

[8]Raine, K. D. *Overweight and Obesity in Canada: A Population Health Perspective*. Centre for Health Promotion Studies, University of Alberta, 2004.

[9]Willet, W. C., W. H. Dietz, and G. A. Colditz. "Guidelines for Healthy Weight," *The New England Journal of Medicine*, Vol. 341, No. 6, August 5, 1999: pp 427-434.

[10]Friedman, A. *Sustainable Residential Developments: Design Principles for Green Communities*. New York: McGraw-Hill, 2007.

Further reading:

Soderstrom, M. *The Walkable City: From Haussmann's Boulevards to Jane Jacobs' Streets and Beyond*. Montreal: Véhicule Press, 2008.

Chapter Thirteen. London's Humility

[1]Mumford, L., *The City in History: Its Origins, Its Transformations, and Its Prospects*. New York: Harcourt, 1961.

[2]Dent, L. *A Survey of Design Codes with Specific Reference to Contemporary Suburban Housing*. Montreal: Unpublished M.Arch. thesis, McGill University Affordable Home Program, July 1993.

[3]Benevolo, L., trans. J. Landry. *The Origins of Modern Town Planning*. Cambridge: MIT Press, 1971.

[4]Stilgoe, J. R. *Borderland. Origins of the American Suburb, 1820-1838*. New Haven: Yale University Press, 1988.

[5]Rogers, I. *Canadian Law of Planning and Zoning*. Toronto: Carswell, 1973.

[6]Haar, C. M. "Reflection on Euclid: Social Contract and Private Purpose." *Zoning and the American Dream: Promises Still to Keep*. Ed. Charles M. Haar and Jerold S. Kayden. Chicago: American Planning Association, 1989.

[7]Feagin, J. R. "Arenas of Conflict: Zoning and Land Use Reform in Critical Political-Economic Perspective." *Zoning and the American Dream: Promises Still to Keep*. Ed. Charles M. Haar and Jerold S. Kayden. Chicago: American Planning Association, 1989.

[9]De Botton, A. *The Architecture of Happiness*. New York: Hamish Hamilton, an imprint of Penguin Books, 2006.

[10]*World Wealth Report 2006*, published by Capgemini and Merrill Lynch, 2006.

Chapter Fourteen. The Soapstones of Iqaluit

[1]Glassie, H. H. *Spirit of Folk Art: The Girard Collection at the Museum of International Folk Art*. New York: Abrams in association with the Museum of New Mexico, Santa Fe, 1995.

[2]Hein, H. *Public Art: Thinking Museums Differently*. Lanham, MD: AltaMira Press, 2006.

[3]Hessel, I. *Inuit Art*. Vancouver: Douglas & McIntyre Ltd., 1998.

[4]Choay, F. *The Invention of the Historic Monument*, trans. L. M. O'Connel. Cambridge, UK: Cambridge University Press, 2001.

[5]Brilliant, R. *Arts of the Ancient Greeks*. New York: McGraw-Hill, 1973.

[6]Becatti, G. *The Art of Ancient Greece and Rome: From the Rise of Greece to the Fall of Rome*. New York: Harry N. Abrams, Inc., 1967.

[7]Aston, M. ed. *The Panorama of the Renaissance*. London: Thames and Hudson, 1996.

[8]Berger, R. W. *Public Access to Art in Paris: A Documentary History from the Middle Ages to 1800*. University Park, PA: The Pennsylvania State University Press, 1999.

[9]Crippa, M. A. *Antoni Gaudí 1852-1926: From Nature to Architecture*. Köln, Germany: Taschen, 2006.

[10]Stirnberg, B. Excerpts from a presentation of his work by the sculptor, at the 1st International M. C. L. Conference, Venice, Italy, 1985.

Further reading:

Dempsey, A. *Destination Art*. Berkeley: University of California Press, 2006.

Chapter Fifteen. Tall Thinking in Amsterdam

[1]Quiney, A. *Town Houses of Medieval Britain*. New Haven: Yale University Press, 2003.

[2]Binney, M. *Town Houses: Urban Houses from 1200 to the Present Day*. New York: Whitney Library of Design, 1998.

[3]Schoenauer, N. *6,000 Years of Housing*. New York: W.W. Norton & Company, 2000.

[4]Guillery, P. *The Small House in Eighteenth-Century London: A Social and Architectural History*. New Haven, London: Yale University Press in association with English Heritage, 2004.

[5]Herman, B. L. *Town House: Architecture and Material Life in the Early American City, 1780-1830*. Chapel Hill: University of North Carolina Press, 2005.

[6]Lockwood, C. *Bricks and Brownstone: The New York Row House, 1783-1929*. New York: Rizzoli, 2003.

[7]Murphy, K. D. *The American Townhouse*. New York: Harry N. Abrams, 2005.

[8]Hayward, M. E., & Belfoure, C. *The Baltimore Rowhouse*. New York: Princeton Architectural Press, 1999.

Further reading:
Friedman, A. *The Grow Home*. Montreal: McGill-Queen's University Press, 2001.
Gorlin, A. *The New American Town House*. New York: Rizzoli, 1999.
Rahbar, M. *Privacy in Row Houses of Montreal*. (Unpublished Master's thesis) McGill University, 1996.

Chapter Sixteen. The Spirit of Assisi

[1]Lane, B. C. *Landscapes of the Sacred: Geography and Narrative in American Spirituality*. Baltimore: The Johns Hopkins University Press, 2002.
[2]Jensen, R. M. *The Substance of Things Seen: Art, Faith, and the Christian Community*. Grand Rapids, MI: William B. Eerdmans Publishing Company, 2004.
[3]Barrie, T. *Spiritual Path, Sacred Place: Myth, Ritual, and Meaning in Architecture*. Boston: Shambhala, 1996.
[4]Cole, D. "Pilgrim's Progress," *National Geographic*, Vol. 213, No. 4, April 2008.
[5]Bergmann, S. *Architecture, Aesthethics & Religion*. Frankfurt: IKO, 2005.
[6]Crippa, M. A. *Antoni Gaudí 1852-1926: From Nature to Architecture*. Köln: Taschen, 2006.
[7]Douthat, R. "Crises of Faith," *The Atlantic*, July/August, 2007. pp. 38-39.

Further reading:
Day, C. *Places of the Soul*. Oxford: Architectural Press, 1990.
Michel, A. *L'Architecture Sacrée*. Paris: Duncan Baird Publishers, 1997.
Norman, E. *The House of God: Church Architecture, Style and History*. London: Thames and Hudson, 1990.
Timothy, D. J. and D. H. Olsen, eds. *Tourism, Religion and Spiritual Journeys*. Oxford: Routledge, 2006.

Acknowledgements

My syndicated column, published since the year 2000 in the CanWest chain of daily newspapers, planted the seed from which this book sprang. A vote of appreciation therefore goes to my editors, and in particular, to Sheila Brady at the Ottawa *Citizen*. Over the years, I have collaborated with a long list of colleagues on research projects which inspired ideas and generated information for the book. I thank them all. Additional research and background information were gathered through the dedicated work of Bori Yoon and Paloma Friedman. Nyd Garavito-Bruhn labored hard to edit and prepare the manuscript for publishing. Thank you. Thanks also go to the McGill School of Architecture for creating an inspiring work environment. Finally, to my family: my wife, Dr. Sorel Friedman, who offered ideas, edited essays, and was my companion in the voyage that led to the experiences described in this book, and to our children, Paloma and Ben.

Illustrations

All images, unless otherwise indicated, were taken by the author.

Frontispiece
A mother holding a child near a fountain, Lucca, Italy.

Teatime in Istanbul
The Istanbul teahouse.

Fiore di Zucchini in Montepulciano
Il matrimonio contadino, a painting by Pieter Bruegel (1525–1569).

Crowding in Hong Kong
Apartment building in Hong Kong.

Turnips in Dalian
The neighborhood market in Dalian.

Hugging in Casole d'Elsa
Strolling up one of Casole d'Elsa's streets.

Swings in Petach Tikva
The Shikun's small park.

Wandering in Tijuana
One of Tijuana's squatter settlement's homes.

E-mail from Broughton Hall
The Pinetum building in Broughton Hall, Skipton, U.K.

The Winds of Fargo
A demonstration igloo in Iqaluit, Nunavut.

The Heart of York
One of York's streets.

The Kitchen of Pina and Felice
A Tuscan landscape near Voltera, Italy.

Pathways in Kfar Sava
A pedestrian mall near the civic centre in Kfar Sava, Israel.

London's Humility
Terrace homes in London, England.

The Soapstone of Iqaluit
A large carving in Iqaluit, Nunavut.

Tall Thinking in Amsterdam
Apartment houses along one of Amsterdam's canals.

The Spirit of Assisi
The Basilica of St. Francis in Assisi, Italy.